Life is Motivation

*If you want to lead the pack,
work harder than the pack*

Connor LaRocque

Copyright © 2014 by Connor LaRocque
First Edition – 2014

ISBN
978-1-4602-4112-7 (Hardcover)
978-1-4602-4113-4 (Paperback)
978-1-4602-4114-1 (eBook)

All rights reserved.

No part of this publication may be reproduced in any form, or by any means, electronic or mechanical, including photocopying, recording, or any information browsing, storage, or retrieval system, without permission in writing from the publisher.

Produced by:

FriesenPress
Suite 300 - 990 Fort St
Victoria, BC, Canada, V8V 3K2

www.friesenpress.com

Distributed to the trade by The Ingram Book Company

Table of Contents

Prologue:
Minimizing excuses, looking for solutions 1

Directing positive energy -
A formula to produce change 11

Chapter 1
Wake up being grateful to be alive
The battle between pain and pleasure 15

Chapter 2
Building confidence and using it as motivation 19

Chapter 3
Building positivity through hope and belief 27

Chapter 4
Revolutionize and enlighten the world 33

Chapter 5
Fate or freewill? 37

Chapter 6
Laziness should never be an option 41

Chapter 7
Encourage people, don't discourage them 47

Chapter 8
Decision making is the ultimate power 51

Chapter 9
We are transformers of our own destiny 53

Chapter 10
Mindset is everything 57

Chapter 11
Prepare to take hits on the battlefield called life 61

Chapter 12
Fear Nothing 65

Chapter 13
Don't base opinions on premature judgment 71

Chapter 14
Equality should be a right not a privilege 75

Chapter 15
Survival of the ego 77

Chapter 16
Darkness is the absence of light, so keep that smile shining bright 81

Chapter 17
You don't have to die to go to Heaven 83

Chapter 18
There will always be doubts in life 85

Chapter 19
The world can be a dark place, but it does not have to be 87

Chapter 20
Just breathe 91

Chapter 21
My story 97

What motivates you? 127

Life is Motivation Poetry
By Connor LaRocque 131

What is life
By Monique LaRocque 133

Inspiring Quotations 135

    Our Mission 136

    Our Objectives 136

    Our History 137

I would like to thank everyone who has been a part of my life and made me the person I am today. Without the support of others, I wouldn't be the love-filled, caring person I am today. I would especially like to thank FriesenPress for taking the initiative and helping me perfect my dream of publishing my book. This is the start of an equality revolution. A movement to help change mindsets.

With these chapters, this book moves into my life story. Once my story is complete you will get to see what other motivated and successful people believe are good techniques to help get them out of bed in the morning.

Dictionary definition of *Impossible:*
Not possible; unable to be, exist, happen, etc.
Unable to be done, performed, effected.

Laugh at this definition because it is meaningless.

Prologue: Minimizing excuses, looking for solutions

The choices you make today dictate your future. You can never go back into a moment because nothing lasts forever. Stand tall and fear nothing because impossible is just an adjective in the dictionary.

Everything that has been created around you started with one thing, which is an idea. The reason I started writing this book is to build a self-sustaining platform to help everyday people. What I have come to realize is that motivation is the essence of life. Motivation is key to life because without motivation, we would die. Motivation is like a power that enables us to unlock a different realm of thought because it excites us to enhance our lives. Obstacles in life only seem difficult because that's how we perceive them to be, but when you look at things honestly, from a different lens, you will surprise yourself with what you are capable of doing. Remember, your life is like a movie except you are the star of this motion picture. I am going to ask various questions throughout this text to help you, the reader, open your mind and allow you to unlock your full potential. With this, you will realize the reality you live in today and how you can transform it. I want **you** to dig deep within your conscious mind and in doing this, change the way you think. If you don't want to read twenty pages in a book, read fifty; that's the mindset I am looking for.

Life is like a ride; it is always moving, changing and generating new experiences—some good, some bad. There is no such thing as motionless reality—unless you're dead! Our bodies and minds are tools that we carry with us every day. They keep the stability of our world intact. As humans, we can only control so much in this volatile world; our attitude and our mindset. The message this book is trying to promote is change, and adapting to change by alleviating fear. Challenging yourself with the things you do not like to do. Breaking mental and physical barriers!

Understand with life comes death, or the afterlife; it is a true mystery. We spend thousands of hours trying to figure out what the meaning of life and death are when this knowledge has been available to us since the dawn of time. It is so simple, yet filled with complexity. However, life is not as complicated as it sometimes seems. It is what you make of it! It is that smile you put on the face of someone who is struggling or starving; it's that hard work and effort you put forth so that one day you will be able to help the masses with no expectation of benefitting yourself. With this life comes disagreement and an ever-growing vicious circle. What people fail to realize is that with extensive effort an ideal utilitarian-style society can be somewhat achieved. How this is done is through everyone helping one another and this will be explained in detail throughout this book.

Humans have a tendency to drive themselves. It runs in the blood of every being known to exist and walk this planet. The fact is, our society is considered weak; we sometimes quit in the face of struggle or don't want to leave the ideal comfort zone, which sets the stage for failure. Evidently, if the body had to perform a task or die, it would find the strength to overcome that adversity. To exceed the odds and revel in the face of a challenge, proving to people who thought the impossible was not possible, is in fact achievable with the right mindset and tenacity.

People like to throw around the word faith and use religion as a key dynamic to pacify the moment, to justify and make themselves feel better. What we are unable to explain becomes clear and that weight is lifted for the short term. The key to turning it from a momentary frame of mind to a long-term discipline is focusing on what the objective is and applying a long-term solution. With this idea, the unknown has meaning rather than incomprehensible complexity.

People who cannot accept the truth will forever struggle in the abyss of their own denial of unanswered questions. I am not saying other forms of life are out there, but in this astonishing universe, there is a possibility of a higher power, something that we can spiritually channel. Something that we cannot experience through the five senses with which we live.

The fact is that we all have something to give, something to share; however, lack of confidence can make giving unachievable. When you believe the non-believers, you become one of them. You become a product of their environment, therefore stopping your development. Frequently it's the person or "self" that is inevitably the weakness. Thousands can believe in what you have to give but unquestionably it all boils down to you, your sense of self that makes a difference.

The reality is that doubt or hesitation will become your worst enemy. The thoughts in your head propel you toward whether you fail or whether you succeed.

If you plan on changing a world, you must be ready to battle precisely to get to the foundation of the problem. In a world filled with people who have no remorse and who operate out of revenge or in constant competition, to reach the top you must be careful. People will stop at nothing to achieve sometimes unattainable goals that serve no great cause. Competition is healthy; greed is not. Competition enables us to push one another to be the absolute best we as people can be. Greed, on the other hand, is filled with selfishness and lust. True happiness is not achieved through greed, happiness is internal, coming from within.

We as humans must use our power to change, to embrace the world thrown in front of us. If psychology has shown us anything, it's that if we take stress as a threat we will break down and quit. But, on the other hand, if we embrace the stress as a challenge in our lifestyle, we will come out stronger and more progressive. Even if we don't come out successful in the tasks performed in life, we will be able to better handle things by getting back up and moving forward without breaking down and quitting. Taking the hits will eventually pay off. The beautiful thing about this life in general is that just when you are about to quit, the magic begins to happen.

We will never progress with a negative perspective on life or thinking that we are better than everybody else. We are all different; therefore making others better at different aspects of their lives, which enables us to help one another. We each interact with thousands of people in our lifetime and if we let the opinions and thoughts of others affect us, it can create mental chaos. We wind up all over the map worrying about how others perceive us. Those who don't listen and don't care how others perceive them are the ones who can reach self-actualization and bring forth peace to this Earth. These people will not get caught up in the little things.

That is not to say we should be inconsiderate to those around us. It means we should listen and exercise those points that are in harmony with our own guiding principles. Those that are not should be discarded. Certain people will understand what life's cards bring to the table and that we can accomplish anything we honestly desire if shown how to. If we wake up in the morning and tell ourselves, "I am going to be the best at making a difference in this world by helping people move forward, including myself," we can, indeed, make a difference. We must stop caring about the criticism of others and start caring about how we are going to make this world a genuinely better place. We all have something within that moves us forward.

That's life's gift to each and everyone one of us, the unknown – being able to create our story and our identity. No one should tell anyone else that they have to be a certain way, although some may try to direct others down the path that they think is best. This is wrong on so many levels because deep down we are who we are. We should not mock others because that is who they genuinely are. Who are we to judge someone who is just being a reflection of how they feel?

We can't continue to use the same solution to every problem because it has worked in the past. The fact of the matter is, it's not always going to work again—this is why throughout history we have created new ideas and innovations, so that we are not stuck with the **same old meat and potatoes.**

People need help. This world was not just built on people crushing one another. At times humans needed other humans to survive, like the French when they first travelled into the unknown through the Northwest Passage on their way to North America. They wouldn't have survived without the Aboriginal peoples. They would have frozen and starved to death. This world was built by people helping each other.

It's the diversity of this world that has helped it expand to where we stand today. Exchanging ideas, importing and exporting things we as people desired and demanded. These are all things that have allowed us to grow exponentially over the last hundred years, whereas before it was a whole different playing field. Maybe Herbert Spencer's idea of survival of the fittest was necessary then, but in this day and age we have the technology and resources available to help one another—not step on one another.

Obviously, some individuals need more help than others because some don't have the proper support mechanisms in place. The point here is that the people who strive for excellence should never forget about helping the people who are in need—those who are legitimately struggling to survive and have too much pride to take money from someone else. Just remember, it's not a good feeling to know people are a suffering and starving while you are enjoying your life.

It's evident that the people who are giving to charities are helping make a difference; however, they need to help promote the same message onto the people who are doing nothing. Those who are successful need to showcase their skills onto others, because they are the people we look up to. Successful people need to show aspiring individuals that they need to give more than they can get. In order to get extraordinary things, you must battle through extraordinary circumstances.

The people we watch on TV and hear about in the news need to help inform others. For them it's positive and promotes good publicity. Who can hate someone if they just want to make a genuine difference? Instead of putting constant fear in people so that we are easier to control and manipulate, why don't we put something on the news worth watching? Something that will make a positive difference? I have a solution that I will go into detail about, and will answer these questions later within these pages.

Fifty years ago, we would never have had to worry about half the ridiculous information that is put in marketing today. Just as Russell Brand points out how people would rather vote for their favorite television stars on TV, rather than political figures running for office. Money is a material possession, whereas caring for another human being is not. Letting people who are struggling starve to death or drink dirty water because all we care about is the size of our bank account shouldn't be an option.

Can you imagine what we could accomplish if we all gave a dollar toward a save the world fund? We would not only gain something powerful, we could achieve something wonderful if put into the proper outlets. We as humans could do something substantial and magnificent. I have helped plenty of struggling people by giving those people ten or twenty dollars and all I can say is that it feels great to see that smile on their faces. It feels better than wasting it on some garbage I do not need. That "thank you" is all I need, nothing else in return. I have never had a more significant natural high than this.

Doesn't it make sense that half the money wasted on advertising could bring people who are struggling a sense of relief and worth? The fact is, some of these kids can't even afford some of the garbage in these commercials. The television practically laughs in their face while they watch.

If I was going to die, I would want someone to save me. Why should we have all this advertisement garbage shoved down our throats? I'm disgusted at the fact that if we advertised something worth our while that we could make a difference, rather than deciding on our choice for lunch. These questions are meant to open each other's minds as to what we are capable of doing. If we've come this far, why can't we change now? Human actions have led to the world today. I believe that we as people are capable of change, that we can make a difference and that we are not just one more fish in the ocean.

When implementing the ability to use our attitudes to benefit us, having high confidence in our capabilities this will allow us to use the power of believing in an idea and ignoring people who will just get in our way. Nothing but keeping an eye on the prize. *History does not repeat itself, because we create it.* History repeats itself when we don't learn from our mistakes the first time, like walking into a wall over and over.

This is not just your world, it's everyone's world, and we are all allowed to partake on this playground—to breathe this air, to feel love, and have a chance to succeed—rather than the idea that we allow people to starve and die being plagued by disease while we sit on the couch flipping through channels.

What's the point of watching people get greedier and laughing in each other's faces because they made it? All this promotes is a negative energy that focuses on hate. This is where helping and sharing comes into play. We need to put our differences aside, stepping into someone else's shoes for once and see the potential we all have instead of allowing this vicious cycle to keep happening—the rich getting richer and poor getting poorer. The middle class deteriorating.

There are plenty of things we do not need, which leaves me to understand that we could give half the possessions we have to someone who has nothing and they would appreciate it much more. The fact is, we are more than capable of doing this. The way we do this is by promoting this new idea and giving up certain things we don't need. We need a global purification, no more intoxication and pollution-causing contamination. The whole idea is that we need to start contributing something that is going to propel this world forward.

If we donate to a bunch of random spaced-out charities, this will not cut it. We need to find something special that will benefit all people in the equation and not just certain areas of need. This is where all the confusion lies, charities now have to compete for funding. We shouldn't just be sitting in awe of the world and mindlessly watching what's going on in front of us. We need to focus and pay attention to what is happening day in and day out. Don't just wonder mindlessly through the day.

We need to take a risk toward something that will come out positively on both sides, even if it fails. It's much better than doing nothing. I will show you that we need to look at both parties' interests rather than just benefiting ourselves. We need to do this for the people who are born into a life of poverty, those stuck working in a factory for a quarter a day.

People from political backgrounds are going to tell you this is impossible, that what I speak of is like comparing apples and oranges. Well the point is, they are incorrect. The fact is that rather than wasting money on desires that benefit slim numbers of the economy, we need a plan of action to benefit the masses, to help change the individualist mindset. Obviously, go for it in life, but we must allow a balance between good and evil. Too much evil is not the answer.

Now that you're starting to understand the reality of this world, the time to change is now, before it's too late and something bad happens and people rebel. What do we do rather than just accept it? Why implement change when it's too late? Why not at least say we tried to do something? It's evident that war doesn't create common ground. It just leaves society in body bags. When society cannot accept change, we kill it. Look at the big hit list: Jesus Christ, Abraham Lincoln, Mahatma Gandhi, Malcolm X, John. F. Kennedy, and Martin Luther King Jr.

All these people promoted a change for the growth of society. There was no selfishness involved but society couldn't accept it and bumped them off. They died for their causes only showing the true powers of their messages.

This is why I cannot understand how we keep watching negative things happen every day without any solutions. Don't worry, I have a solution. Contribute to the right sections of society, absorb as much free knowledge from the Internet and books as possible, because it's as valuable as anything. Expand your mind by reading, promoting yourself and your message in a way that people can grasp.

Have a strategy to reach the success you would like to achieve. If it does not work, then switch your strategy. For example, if you are trying to remember something, use cues such as letters or acronyms to help trigger something in your brain. I will explain these techniques in more detail throughout this book. It will leave us to think, "How can we just sit on the sidelines making observations and accept this is how it's going to be?" Change your vocabulary if it's reflecting negative results in your life. Why? Because vocabulary is a tool we use to make connections and understand things. If you are always negative, you would be surprised what a few words could do to brighten your day! Words frame mental pictures, allowing you to interpret things.

We can put whatever label we want on it, but the facts do not lie. No person wants to clean up the mess that was started centuries ago because we are scared of the challenge. We do not want to work for it, but to actualize this goal, we must see that it can be achieved. It's significant that some have tried and failed because we are not promoting this message properly. We need to get into one another's heads the same way the media does to sell a product. Or we can use the same techniques employed to implement fear into our bodies and minds. We must subconsciously encode it within our brains.

How did a person like Adolf Hitler control mass numbers of people promoting nothing but the negative? Why can't a significant number of strong-minded believers do the same, but promote a positive message? **The fact is, we can**. Hitler proved this, but he did something horrible. So let's come together to do the right thing. I will show you the way but you must start by using your time effectively because it's the most valuable commodity. In chapter two, I will teach you how to believe in yourself and build confidence. Once you understand this, you will then be able to take on the world, seeing it in a new light.

Its simple logic—we must "do" rather than "don't". There is too much of this "don't" attitude winning the battle. I used to sit and think too much rather than just doing something. Occupying your time is by far the best solution to anything. Like Forest Gump said, "I just start running." The people who are not doing enough with their lives, who are feeling as if they should be doing more, need to get in motion and get this party started. Find your passion! Find what gives you that natural rush and makes you smile!

We must always give back and then grasp how much of a difference this makes, even if it is a small difference. It is going to be a start toward something great. In my psychology class, six out of one-hundred and ten students put up our hands to say they have contributed to a charity. Be the person who promotes change—the visionary and positive thinker, not the person who has a hard time wrapping their head around what they're going to do in their spare time. Some of the most successful people in the world say time is of the essence, so don't waste it. Go a full day without being negative; this will cause you to be positive and it eventually become habitual. Once it is habitual, it will become second nature. If something is negative, use your thoughts to direct your energy and focus on something positive.

All knowledge is potential power. Don't be the person who wonders years down the line why they didn't accomplish something. Work hard, set goals, and achieve them. It all starts with a positive fearless attitude. Realize that it's much better to regret doing something than not doing it at all. Start by being prepared for anything the world throws at you and be ready to promote change on a global level. With this in mind, negatives should not even be a part of your vocabulary. Take out words such as "cant" "if" or "but" and replace them with words such as "can" and "will".

If nobody has your back, always know that at least you have your own back. Don't stop promoting the greatness of mankind. People will eventually see and interpret the message you are trying to promote. Surprise yourself and come to terms with what you are capable of doing. Don't lay alone in the abyss of your own thoughts. Take the ideas from your mind and bring them into physical reality by writing them down on paper.

Always remember it is much easier to achieve a goal when you know exactly what you want or have a general idea. If you are just working toward something blindly in the stars, it is much harder than if you are working toward getting to the moon.

The future will not change if we do not let it—in the following chapters I will tell you the story of my life and you will understand the potential we all possess. Every chapter includes something that will enable you to become a more positive, helping person. The words that follow will help answer some of life's toughest questions that each and every one of us ask ourselves. I will showcase some of the various techniques you can use to make your thoughts a reality. Follow the guidance in these chapters and it will allow you to see light where there is darkness. It will be encoded into your brain functioning that by the end of this book anything and everything will be positive in some way or another. Certainty is the key to making this a reality. If you are uncertain about something, it will affect you in a negative way. Whereas, if you are certain about something where no one has ever walked before you will be able to walk through the flames of life with confidence. I find with people in general the only reason some do not like to read is the fact that they have never found anything of interest to themselves or lured them into continuing.

Decision, Certainty, Fear, Judgment and Passion. These five variables will define who you are and what you stand for either positively or negatively.

Directing positive energy - A formula to produce change

Action 1:

You need a plan of action, a strategy that you can work with. Something that is going to bring you pleasure after it is achieved. Example: A plan to save 1000 dollars and how to budget it properly. Take 100 off the top off every paycheck and give yourself a date for when this will be met. If you can't take 100 every paycheck, balance your plan so that you will be able to meet your deadline. Weigh the pros and cons, pains and pleasures that this plan is going to bring forth.

Action 2:

You need to figure out what exactly it is you want so you will be able to aim in that general direction. With this, you must picture it in your mind. Once you figure out what it is that you want to do, research your topic of interest and gain as much knowledge about it as you possibly can. Example: If you want to become a lawyer, then research what has to be done to be the best one possible. What marks do you need? What are the associated costs? What's the best school? What law firms and people can you speak with to gain the most valuable advice?

Action 3:

Start allowing your thoughts, emotions, and actions to intertwine with this strategy and feel the energy they produce. If one of these three variables falls out of line, use the other two for balance. Example: If your thoughts are not reflecting your actions, then change your thoughts to reflect your actions. If you think you can't do something, attempt it on a smaller scale and test yourself. Let your actions speak, not your thoughts. If your emotions are taking over and you want to get angry, use your actions and thoughts to keep telling yourself you are going to be all right, taking deep breaths so you can focus. Do not give into the neurochemical imbalance in brain.

Action 4:

Lay a foundation for success by asking yourself where you see yourself in a year from when this strategy is set. Then five years, and finally ten. Example: Sit somewhere by yourself and focus. Go deep within your mind and play all the possibilities out. Determine where you may have issues and prepare for them.

Action 5:

Prepare for the road ahead and the possible adjustments that may need to be made. Do not just give up on your idea. Ask yourself, do I really want this? If yes, make the adjustments. If not, ask yourself if it is because it's too hard or because you seriously do not want it bad enough. This will lead you where you need to go. Repeat this cycle with whatever you desire in this lifetime. Even with the most basic things, it will help provide structure. Before you know it, you will have an indestructible strategy. Remember, failure is just temporary and in having effective goals, you will always have something to look forward to, which is key to building motivation. NOW TEST IT!

Chapter 1
Wake up being grateful to be alive
The battle between pain and pleasure.

The day starts when you get up in the morning. You may be tired, weak, and not want to get out of bed to continue your everyday routine, but you need to understand if you can get up, you've beat the first mental battle of the day. Plant your feet, get to work, and be productive. It's understandable that mornings are when we may be at our weakest, but this is when just getting those feet in gear helps.

Take a cold shower or splash water on your face if you need to get yourself up; just don't let life bring you down. Always remember someone else out there has a much harder life than you do and would give anything to be in your position. If you can't get out of bed, you must not want to become successful bad enough.

Use this as motivation to better yourself. Don't consider what you would like to have, but rather consider what you do have to give and be grateful for it.

People are at times greedy and want more than they need, when there are people out there who would love to just have something rather than nothing. You should want to see others' progress, just as you aspire to. Of course, you want success just as much as the next person does—just stay humble about what you are reaching for and always give back.

If you're having a bad day, just remember that you can always pick up where you left off tomorrow. If you become bored, keep your mind occupied and do something—don't just stare at the wall. It's reasonable that this can be hard but it's just your psyche playing tricks on you. There will always be something to do to keep you occupied. Just do anything—go for a jog, read a book, call someone. The best thing to do is to search the Internet for things that can help you enhance your knowledge. Just ensure it is scholarly information! This is what I enjoy doing: finding things I'm interested in to expand my mind rather than sitting on Facebook or other forms of social networking. Distractions, as I like to call them.

If you spend all your time living in regression, you will drive yourself into a constant depression. You are in control - you have the power: just believe it - don't be hopeless.

Just think: hundreds of years ago people didn't have anything close to the technology this world has today to keep them occupied, so you should have plenty to do. Learn to program your brain to do things you are not accustomed to and things you don't like to do. Learn to enjoy reacting in different situations you are not accustomed to so you're capable of doing anything and not surprised when change hits you. Make a game out of it—life's a game, except it's your video game. Go talk to someone, or take a chance you usually wouldn't. You can always sharpen a tool or make improvements to minor things even if this means adjusting your ego.

Get up in the morning ready to go to war with life in a positive manner—not aggressively, but attack life as if you had no choice but to make a difference. Why take the easy way out in life when the hard road is the way to reality and not fantasy? Life is hard if you let it be. Failure is not an option; it's just the easiest way out. Many people will turn to failure because they don't want to put in the hard work and effort. They look for a shortcut to make things easier when the only way to do things properly is to do it right. Easy tasks don't teach us much; it's the harder tasks that pose a challenge. If something is always the same, you will never grow as a person. It's the changes throughout life that enable us to grow.

Would you rather fail by quitting, or fail because you gave it your all and that wasn't enough? You are not a quitter but a go-getter, looking failure in the eyes and laughing because you will never break.

Even if you do break, you will learn from the experience and it will never happen again because you have been there before. We are given a body and a brain, so use your tools effectively.

Life is Motivation

I want you, the reader, to realize that everything we as humans do is not based on intelligence but rather pain and pleasure. This is how we measure if we want to do something or not. Some people will suffer the pain of a workout to become stronger, while others would rather not put themselves through the pain, so instead they indulge in the pleasure of laziness. Tony Robbins made this concept clear to me and it in fact showcases why we as humans do what we do. Another example is if we do not want to go on a diet because we think it will be too painful, and instead take the short-term pleasure of not enduring the pain of dieting. When you make a decision, be conscious of how these two variables effect your life.

Isn't it ironic how successful people got to where they are today with hard work and not just sheer luck? It's the people with the negative outlook who will use this analogy as an excuse as to why they are unable to perform as others do. It's just a defense mechanism to support why they don't want to do something. It's like the people who are glued to their cellphones and won't make eye contact—it's a defense mechanism to back up the fact that they don't want to participate in something Think about this for a second—the people who are usually considered lucky are the ones with a plan and drive forward with tenacity.

Do you want to be one of these people, shy and afraid, or do you want to understand that you can walk into a room and be equal? We are all equal as humans in that we are given a body and brain; we bleed and breathe. We are all equally sharing the amount of air we breathe. Minimize excuses and think to yourself why you are not performing at your full potential.

Don't think that for one minute the most successful people in the world don't use defense mechanisms, it's just that they have learned from their mistakes the first time so they perform differently the next. Make the minor adjustments needed so that you are not questioning your performance in life. Be critical of yourself. This is why the hard way out will help you understand life as well as provide more of an appreciation for life. Remember, the premise of this book is that YOU have the power to change the masses—just see it and believe it, I will show you how.

Even the elite have room for improvements, working out minor mistakes so that a technique is mastered. This happens by means of hard work not an "easy way out" mentality.

Chapter 2
Building confidence and using it as motivation

One of the major things that leads to failure in the real world is lack of confidence. I am going to speak about this throughout this whole book because it has driven many people to the brink of failure, when it is, in fact, a fallacy. The problem is, where do you start? I like to say that it's all about having belief in yourself, but how do you get that? How do you build confidence and live with a fearless attitude?

It all starts when you look yourself in the mirror and say, "I am no better than anybody." The fact is, you have many skills and abilities that can compare to anyone's. So you're overweight and scared that people are judging you? Just because society says that's not the way you're supposed to be, does that make people who are not overweight better than you? No, it doesn't at all—that's the point. Society tries to tell us how we should act and what we should say. For the person looking to build confidence, if they believe people on television or that Photoshopped images are real, it's not going to help you.

The best answer to helping yourself is having will power, not taking "good enough" as an answer. You need to look at yourself and understand that you make mistakes, but not to feel sorry for yourself. Instead, do something to change the way you are feeling. If you are having a hard time with things, it's a matter of switching mental cognition.

What I mean by this, is say to yourself one hundred times, "I am great, I believe in myself," even if you don't. You have to do this to get your mind off the negative—that you think your weak, overweight, or are unable to do something. Even if you are not able to do something, tell yourself you can do it, then attempt it. If you keep telling yourself negative things that make you feel worse, it will drag you down even further.

This is why you have to tell yourself, "I am changing, I am confident." Scream it if you have to. I do not want you to walk into a room and feel scared of being judged—besides, who is the person to be judging you in the first place? That person doesn't even know you, so how can he or she judge you? Or maybe that person knows you, but still, how can they do that? When this happens, use it as motivation. Just because someone you don't even know is judging you, why are you going to let that bring you down when you are working toward a goal?

The fact is that it is our human nature, which has a tendency to observe and judge others around us. The only difference is, it is our perception that can allow us to make connections and the fundamental changes to not negatively look at someone.

This is where building confidence starts. It starts by you knowing you have a high self-worth, that you are no different from anybody else in the sense that you have a brain, a body, bleed, and breath. In my experience being fat growing up, I was already self-conscious about my weight and focused on how hard it was to lose weight. I didn't lose the weight because it was much easier indulging in the pleasure of laziness and not committing to a program. Plus, I didn't want it bad enough. You have to want it so bad that you become obsessive over it. You can practically see yourself achieving the goal and living the reality. When I listened to other people, it just upset me more. The only person who could change my self-worth was me. I had to find something that I enjoyed and could work at that allowed me to build confidence. I had to ask myself, do I really want to change? In doing this, I was committing to a program.

The two variables that hurt people who are trying to commit to a program are consistency and persistence. If you aren't consistent you will not see the results you would like, as well if you are not persistent you will not continue on with your routine, especially if you are having a bad day.

For me it was martial arts, but for others it could be anything from a sport to art or writing. Something that will enable you to express yourself. We all as people have something that gives us pleasure. We need techniques to be able to ignore the negative doubters. If they bring something negative to you, like "you will never change", prove them wrong. Don't sit there and let them pick at you, but instead keep moving forward, knowing that in the end you will have the last laugh. Use whatever negative things people feed you to motivate you to take a plan of action. Set your goal, strategize a plan on how you are going to achieve it, then chip away at it until you reach it.

You need to change the way you think if you worry about others judging you. Whenever you feel the onslaught of a bad thought, say to yourself, "No, I am confident. I am working toward a goal and I believe in myself." It's this idea that this whole book revolves around. If you dread doing something, it's only going to make it worse. That's why you have to get excited to do things you don't enjoy. You hate doing math or editing, then tell yourself you love it, that it's going to make you better. Ask yourself, "What am I doing to better myself?" If you keep feeling sorry for yourself or saying negative things to yourself, how do you expect to rise up out of the situation?

Rather than making excuses, tell yourself positive things by setting a goal and working toward it. This builds confidence and enables you to have something to look forward to. This will excite you at the same time rather than dreading something. Even if you're not successful today, you will be one day as long as you stay positive, no matter what the circumstance. Failure is positive because at least you are attempting to succeed. Just don't stop until you succeed. Live and learn. Make succeeding your goal or at least attempting something because that in itself is an accomplishment. Like Zig Ziglar says "You have to be a dreamer."

Believe to achieve.

Understand that in order to build confidence, no matter what happens to you in your life, no matter how stressed you are, at least you can smile and know eventually everything is going to be all right. Look yourself in the mirror and smile, even if you see terror in your eyes—your smile may be the only thing to bring you back in check. Even if you are still upset, show yourself you can be happy even if you aren't (trick your brain).

It may take a couple of hours or a couple of days, but your smile will keep that eternal flame burning strong inside of you. Just think, you are not going to feel that way forever. Certain things are going to bring you down, but it's your job to pick yourself back up and not let yourself take over. When things are broken, we fix them. This same concept applies for life and reality. Don't keep crying; get back on that horse, never backing down, and I'm almost certain your mind will surprise you with what it is capable of doing.

We have heard the example of people finding supernatural strength in times of struggle, then find out later they saved someone and did something unnatural, such as lifting up a car or pulling a child out from underneath something. Use this strength that's deep inside you to overcome the impossible and beat whatever is taking over you. Lift yourself up to the heights you once were. You must slowly take small steps every single day towards facing your fears. Start vocalizing your opinions in conversations, if you're scared of heights go to the local diving towers and face your fear. Whatever it is that makes you scared, there will be a way to attempt it on a smaller scale. You need to remember, we are all human, we all go about our day—so if someone looks at you differently that's okay.

Let the tears dry and vanquish your fears, even if you think it's not possible, because it is.

For instance, look at people who drop hundreds of pounds of weight. It may look impossible, but it's done every day and those people deserve gratitude for helping motivate the people who are trying to lose weight.

We must not yield ourselves to "I can't". We must open our minds to the true greatness that can be accomplished through patience and constant hard work to complete a goal. Yes, life may get boring and repetitive at times, but this is the way it has to be to perfect greatness. It's not time to quit and move on to something else when we become bored. It is the long-term goals that provide happiness, not the short-term instant gratification. We must work harder, knowing in the long term that the mission will be complete. Our globalized society is moving at a very fast pace, the internet allows us to get things in an instant. The problem with this is that success doesn't follow the same natural laws—success takes time, hard work, daily goals and an unstoppable mindset. If you don't have a mission, figure one out and attack it. Find something you want to do and start drilling towards it, day in and day out. Eat, sleep and breathe that idea. Make something out of your time. We have twenty-four hours in a day; eight of that is sleeping, the other ten is working, one hour is eating and the rest is up to you.

Being bored is another weakness that brings people down. The onset of boredom should be a signal to turn it into a positive by doing something that expands knowledge and acts as a springboard to keep us moving forward. Sitting in a spot doing absolutely nothing creates boredom. With this, we must have patience too, because success will not come overnight. It takes dedication, time, and hard work to do great things.

Hundreds of years ago, life was much more difficult than it is now. Fear was at an all-time high and people had to live day by day. There was no time for boredom. There was time to work to support your family while people somewhat understood the right value system.

Today, there are too many options and as a society, we are moving in the wrong direction. We don't have to fight for our survival or have to worry about our head getting thrust into a guillotine. This leaves me to point out the fact that our society in general has a weak mindset towards the ongoing problems and arising ones. We quit in the face of a struggle because we think that something is too difficult, when hundreds of years ago it was a much more difficult living environment—either do or die. Like the wolf in the wild, either live or die.

We are in the safest environment we have ever been and it is time to start acting like it, rather than buying into all the drama that is constantly portrayed. There are always going to be problems—this is reality. Whether a person deals with problems negatively or positively is a choice.

Life can always be rebuilt after the hurricane has hit. When you see struggles happening around you, don't just accept it, try something new and change your approach—you may have a better view. I may repeat this idea about being positive because it works. I want it to be encoded into your brain that when you start thinking negatively you will say, "Let's try something new."

Mainstream media blasts people with negatives such as the next big threat or war going on—all just garbage with no positivity. This is fed by what society wants to hear or read (drama sells). Look at all these new workout supplements or machines that marketers claim can make you fit by working out twenty minutes a day. The funny thing is, you have to eat right and be consistent for this to happen, but the TV ads neglect to mention this.

Another example: if a new form of cancer surfaces, then show people things that can help prevent cancer, whether it's certain foods or other things we can avoid. Worrying creates nothing but negativity! It does nothing but cause stress and creates a bad outcome. Imagine how you would feel not knowing you had cancer, then the drastic change that would happen when you find out you have it. On top of all that, the doctor playing god and saying you have three months to live. Imagine how that would affect you mentally.

This coils back to the idea of fear and how it's able to control us. If we have a negative, worrying attitude about what's going on around us, it will do nothing but make matters worse. But if we think the opposite with a positive attitude and desire to challenge the obstacles thrown in front of us, we will most certainly come out with better results. I can only imagine if I had had confidence in myself rather than being extremely self-conscious growing up.

There is nothing wrong with being highly confident in ourselves, provided we can back it up. I had to recognize that I was the same as everybody else and that I had the same self-worth. No one can say what you are worth but you. If you listen to every negative opinion, the impact on your confidence will be negative. There is nothing wrong with constructive criticism; however, rather than ignoring the irrelevant information people feed you, use their criticism to better yourself by increasing your self-worth.

Whatever you desire, make it a compulsion; encode it within your subconscious realm by thinking about it constantly and don't stop till it's achieved. Always have it on your mind. If you get knocked down, get back up. I can't emphasize this enough. Everyone makes excuses, but you can look anywhere in the world and find someone who has a much harder life—what's your excuse? Your back is sore. Well, there are top-level athletes in the Special Olympics who have it much harder.

Write down on a card what you would like to have, whether it's money, success, or helping promote your message. Keep it with you every single day and look at it regularly, instilling it in your mind. This will bring your dreams into physical reality.

Don't hesitate to self-talk and use affirmations. Believe in yourself, because as I said before, it all boils down to you. If you let others pick at you and get to you, you will become a product of their environment.

If someone like Fredrick Douglas (a famous slave who started a local newspaper) can realize he is great in a time of mass slavery when everyone told him he was nothing but property, then we as people should have no problem coming to the conclusion that we can all make a difference if we put our minds to it. Know that the more we do not rely on others, the easier things will become. There will not be that constant stress to give something back or that we owe someone. We remain independent. Self-reliance is ideal. Now repeat, "I am equal, I can do anything." Remember, as soon as someone judges or negatively influences you, use positive reinforcement to tell yourself otherwise. Do not let negative thoughts haunt your brain and cause you distress. Rather, laugh in the face a challenge.

Chapter 3
Building positivity through hope and belief

Don't tell me the sky's the limit when there are footprints on the moon. - Brandt Paul

There is too much doubt and not enough belief in this world. Often good ideas get thrown away because of lack of confidence. We need to come to realize that if we just keep our ideas on the surface, they will not have true meaning. Don't let your ideas be forgotten and fade into the waves of the ocean. If others doubt you, understand that it could be because of jealousy or other underlying factors.

If you are willing to take a risk and possibly accept failure or reap the rewards, nothing can hurt you. Don't let other people bring your ideas down. Why let someone hurt you when you are happy?

Even if you think your idea is not one hundred percent perfected, you can still work with it. Thomas Edison didn't invent the light bulb the first time, so avoid letting negativity chip away at you. You and only you will be able to know when you are ready to present an idea. You will feel that spark of energy that brings joy to you because you know you have something special and want it to shine bright.

Ask yourself, why do people quit on themselves? It's because they do not believe. Well, what believing means is to have certainty. Understand people become tired and break down, doubting their idea or themselves. The go getters will run that extra mile and take that risk even if they might fail. Ultimately, they believe in themselves and their idea. They are able to let their inner spirit guide them toward achieving their goal while not letting others lead them off course. The word believe has "lie" in it, so even if you have to tell yourself things that have false premises, do so to keep you moving.

When you are in the zone, your body just reacts. The mind and body connection is so powerful that you do not even have to think, you just operate. Like how one foot walks in front of the other without thought. Use this power to believe in not only yourself but the ideas you would like to present. Let it boost your confidence and make you a better person, rather than letting negativity stab you in the back. React, react, and react.

This world is a beautiful place, not one where you should have to worry about being judged or criticized for your ideas because of who you are. We are all different to some extent, but equal in the sense that all we want is security and a chance to succeed.

If you don't believe in yourself, who will?

I don't care who you are, at some point life will hit you like a bus, whether it be through tragedy, death, or despair. There will always be circumstances that will affect our lives in traumatic ways. There is no control over this. Wouldn't it be wonderful if you could live the perfect life? The reality is there are always going to be bumps in the road. Don't think that there will not be sad days because this is all part of the game of life. Life at times may overwhelm you, it may bring you down to your lowest hour, but you must hold your head high and stay strong so that you can battle through this adversity. If you cannot move forward and are having a hard time with life, you must find a way to regain that strength that once put a smile on your face.

Go back to something you love doing and get your mind thinking differently. Break out of this dark hole we call depression and stand tall. Obviously, in some cases depression will take over, it will become you. But you can use your power to change, to adjust your attitude. It's all about mental strength. You must find what motivates you deep down, something that you love (such as sports, art, etc.). You are what you think; therefore, you can become exactly what you would like to be. Meaning, you can put a smile on the face of a frown. This may sound farfetched, but after a time of tragedy, you will come to terms with the idea that this can legitimately be beneficial and help you. It can make you a stronger person because you are able to control your emotions. Change your vocabulary to reflect the way you want to feel. For example, if you are tired, tell yourself you are rather "uncomfortable" and so on.

In some cases, it may not seem like an option, but if we are unable to try then how can we know if it will work or not? If we have done nothing to change what we are feeling, how can we say we are at least trying to help ourselves? New days are better days—scars heal as time fades into the sunset. Seek someone with who you have a connection, who will be able to give you your strength back. Someone who will enable you to see that light at the end of the tunnel to let go of some of that built up stress and negative emotion.

With depression is this idea of death, which may seem like a negative when it is a positive. It enables us to realize we only have so much time to perfect our goals—it gives us motivation. When someone in your life dies, always remember that they wouldn't want to see you crying, they would want to see you be the best you can be. They would also want you to use their death as motivation to do something, to give you a spark. You can want to change depression, but the only way to do so is through adjusting your attitude and perception.

Whether this means talking to someone, working out, or meditating, it will assist you in alleviating this pain. Would you rather be depressed for the rest of your life, or be happy so that you can enjoy the time you have here? You are going to be deceased longer than you are alive. Negativity and stress are killers.

Death is the worst thing that happens on the Earth, but it is a positive in that it makes you stronger. It can open up your eyes and can enable you to see a new perspective. This will allow you to understand how important not wasting time is and how to manage it properly. Understand that sometimes life hits so hard that all you have is hope; hope for a better tomorrow, hope for that smile once again, hope that one day everything will work out as planned. If you give up on hope, what else do you have besides a negative energy that is just going to bring you down even further, sucking the life right out of you? People can say hope is a fallacy, but I don't understand how someone can say this. What are struggling people supposed to do, just accept death, or give themselves something that can help them grow or feel something positive?

Do you not think starving children in Ethiopia do not hope for a better tomorrow or for clean water? Or that children of war do not hope that one day their life is going to be alright? We the people must fill this void so that these children can at least have something more than hope. We must fill the void in the hearts of the people suffering from struggle and despair. We must take action, guiding people who do not understand or want to help and show them success can be reached with a goal and belief in it.

We need to change in order for humanity to progress. Using the same tactics in battle over and over doesn't work because eventually they become outdated. Giving up a present on Christmas would illustrate a different perspective people would see (I gave all my Christmas money to charity because the kids who don't have anything deserve to enjoy a Christmas more than me). Or giving up something you enjoy so that you can at least put a smile on the face of someone who is struggling.

These are tactics that change how people think, and make them think twice about what they are doing.

By helping a family in need you will not only help better their lives, but your own as well. It feels good to know you have made a difference to someone with something that you place very little value to yourself but means the world to someone else. We need to start somewhere and these little things are a step in the right direction. They can cause a chain reaction and turn into big things, once people start to see and realize the endless possibilities. It's called the compound effect. The continuous repetition of habits that form the lifestyle you will live.

Enlightenment can be started from something small. It just takes other people to see it and have the right leadership skills in place to push it in the right direction, which will gain followers. People who are going to risk being judged. Research something, a cause that interests you that you know you can help with, even if it means taking little steps. Know YOU can make a difference.

Throughout history, it is evident that all you need is an idea; something to promote and market well enough so that people will be able to understand. Like a food commercial, we must get people to want it, to do anything to get it, to stop at nothing or for no one. By doing nothing, how is a goal to be reached?

It's hard work, persistence, and person with a plan that can put a dent in the idea that something is impossible. This needs to be done for the citizens who do not have anything, who are in need of help. The smallest of things can make a difference, you just have to understand and believe this. Believe in the change. Start by promoting some type of change, do something to get the people's attention. Show people that anything is possible, nothing is to unrealistic. If you feel it can be done, then challenge yourself and see if you are wrong. Do me a favor, JUST START. How? Lay a blue print, research what needs to be done to accumulate the success you are looking to achieve. In doing this, look at how other individuals achieved what you what. If no other individual has walked were you want to go, then find your route of access.

Chapter 4
Revolutionize and enlighten the world

"We as people all see the world through a different lens, this is why we can gain terminal knowledge from anyone we interact with." If you are able to see the wrong in the world, don't just sit there and accept it. Try to at least do something to fix it, rather than letting it progress. Contribute more to charity, help people and better things will come forth. It's clear that talk is cheap—it's the actions that matter. A "comment" or "like" on Facebook is not going to make a difference; donating a dollar to charity will.

However, if everyone was to add their own piece to the puzzle, anything could happen. Imagine what would happen if all the money we spend on warfare and protection was spent on charity. Even if every person you know contributed a dollar to a specific fund to promote peace, a positive change would be felt, rather than the negative of nothing happening. This stupid idea portrayed that our world is falling apart and people are hopeless. I wouldn't care if I was falling off a cliff, I would still think to myself, "I am going to survive." That's how powerful my belief is in promoting change.

It only takes one idea to spark greatness, so let the bandwagon effect take place. Once again, ignore the doubters who think it is impossible. They will just stand in the way that you need to go. If you have certainty, see where it will take you. Sometimes negative consequences can be for the better, as long as you have a conglomerate of people standing behind you who will promote your idea. If Abraham Lincoln did not promote his idea that everyone thought was negative, others may not have realized that what he was doing was actually positive and what everyone else was doing was wrong (not freeing the slaves).

Don't be scared to promote something, be prepared.

Steve Jobs (Apple Computer's CEO, inventor and entrepreneur) was a great example of the idea that we as humans must grow, that when you have an idea, you can make it even better. He did this in the right context to push people to help them unlock there true potential—realizing that you can always fix something and make improvements. Things may not be seen as clearly until this potential is reached and a person's eyes become opened.

By revolutionizing the way people think and conversing with one another, a positive energy is created. Don't let the ignorance of people affect your performance and positive vibe—just laugh and use your tools to try and make them feel better. If this does not work, they will eventually come to terms with themselves. You can only put a smile on the faces of people who care (this doesn't mean you don't at least try). Don't worry about the micro things in life—they will drive you nuts. The macro things are the primary focus. Someone being rude to you because they are having a bad day shouldn't even faze you.

If you know you're promoting peace, happiness, and excellence, don't worry about others who are unable to comprehend this; let them live in a world filled with ignorance and hatred. Eventually they may see the change and come to terms. Revolutionizing the world in front of you, enlightening people by being a more positive and enthusiastic person, will rub off on others. Encourage, encourage, encourage. Don't look down on people because you have not taken steps in their shoes, as they haven't in yours. Be the most positive person in the room, what's of matter if people think you are to much.

What is the one thing a person who is disturbed does not like? When you are smiling and happy. Rather than figuring out their situation, they will do anything to take that smile away from you because they are miserable. Smiles are contagious. It's all about looking on the bright side, always looking for a way out and not accepting something if you seriously are not happy. Take this example: you have a friend who is always depressed and brings everyone down. What do you do? You don't just sit there and let them be negative, ask them questions that will try to help them figure out their situation.

See if you can help trigger a new outlook in the person's life and make them realize a minor change can be made. Don't always think to yourself, "Yeah, they're negative." Try to help them out unless they don't want help. Mention a little stress relief like a sport could help. Give them a hug reassure them that everything is going to be okay as long as they believe so. Tell that person if they don't believe, they may find it difficult to ever change their attitude.

Being someone who thinks they know everything is impossible because we as humans can never rationally understand everything. Every day we learn and grasp new ideas that will change our outlook from the day that came before, enhancing our knowledge. In a sense, we grow and become smarter day by day. Education is addicting in my opinion.

Jesus Christ is a perfect example to look up to because he would go around discussing new ideas with people and try to give them insight and a different perspective of the world, to help people better understand life and the beauty of it. Don't be scared to be criticized or judged. If we never receive criticism, how are we able to fix our mistakes to better our knowledge? If you are unable to take criticism, how are you able to dish it out? Just remember, someone is trying to help fix minor mistakes when they criticize you so that you can make minor adjustments for the future.

Whether it's your golf swing or hockey slap shot, positive criticism can enhance your skills so that you are able to do better next time. But watch out, sometimes people may not know what they are talking about. If you see everyone doing it this way, then it is probably the right way. People involved in the field you are working in will surely know if you are doing things properly, not the individual who thinks they have perfected everything. You may have your own techniques that you have learned and this is okay; just compare both ideas so that you are able to do whatever it is you are doing efficiently. Look at in martial arts how Bruce Lee emphasized doing what works most efficient for yourself. Why? Because he understood we are all different, which means we have different strengths and weaknesses. Learning from professionals is the best way to do anything because they have been there and done that; they've put the hard work in to achieve the success they have today. Another example is the flawed school system teaching kids that their usually is only one answer to a question. Or how school teachers you not to make mistakes when the reality is that making mistakes is the only way to learn. You could be an A student in school but when it comes to facing obstacles lack some of the physical "real world" skills. It is always good to learn about conceptual things, just apply them to the real world. That's how you will revolutionize and enlighten everyday life. By learning new things and applying them to the real world.

My point is, learning from your mistakes in life can revolutionize and enlighten the way you think. This will allow you more points of reference within your thought process, which in terms will give you more experience. If someone keeps barking in your ear about something, don't get frustrated. Take a step back and wonder to yourself why you keep getting questioned. You may be surprised to find that on video it looks different than what you pictured in your head. I used to hate being criticized, it only frustrated me, but the reality was it made me that much better, stronger, and more efficient at what I was doing. The people you are working with to perform certain tasks are there to see you succeed, so a little criticism never hurt anybody. You can't expect to have perfected everything. There will always be minor work that can be done.

Overall, we as humans never stop learning and absorbing from each other. Everyone has a different perspective on this world. We all see the world differently so there will always be different ways to look at something to change your perception. Don't be surprised that you may see something differently than others. Always picture a mirrored image of yourself not from your angle, but from how others may perceive you.

Eat up knowledge; be excited to learn, because learning is a great thing. Time to enlighten the world. Pick up a book not the TV converter. - Connor LaRocque

Chapter 5
Fate or freewill?

Like all great works of art, there must be an artist.

I'm not saying you have to be religious, it's just that faith has helped me in my life even when there were doubts. There are always going to be doubts in this empirical world because the reality is, we do not know exactly how we got here (even though we have a good idea). I have nothing against atheists; I just believe that their view of the world is limited with no spirituality. Atheists place faith in scientific data even though they don't like to believe so. I also believe we cannot just rely on our five senses. There are sound frequencies we cannot hear, there are things such as atoms we cannot see and so on.

In a place that is so grand with so many unexplainable things, it is hard to believe that there is nothing else out there. Just looking up in the night sky seeing all these unknown planets as well as stars that are unexplored and not fully understood leaves room for thought. My idea is that we limit ourselves by thinking inside the box rather than outside the box. Although this is an overused philosophical saying, the context I am using this analogy in is different.

Consider my example that explains this reality: if we were to be taken outside this world, looking down at the Earth and its huge mass, it would almost be terrifying in my opinion. Why? Because in our lifetimes, we have never seen anything that colossal. No ocean, no mountain. It would almost be overwhelming to comprehend. It would be the biggest thing our small bodies have ever seen.

What this goes to show you is that this universe is much bigger than what we perceive here on Earth and that leaves me to think that there is a possibility of something else being out there. Imagine seeing Jupiter with your own eyes. Just think, there are definitely stars bigger than Jupiter.

I am not saying God is out there, but it is definitely a possibility that we cannot discount. Like Albert Einstein said: "We cannot see air, yet it exists." This leads me to point out that I graduated from a Catholic school, and you know what it taught me? How corrupt some of these religions are by breaking their own morals and fighting for what they believe is the correct idea. In my opinion, I wasn't a believer due to a Catholic high school and all of the history I learned from it. It took me years to determine that we all want the same thing, which is **an answer**, something that is going to explain how we got here and why we exist.

Every religion promotes a similar basic premise that they believe in something and want to help people by enlightening them. All religions tend to worship the same God, whether the name changes or whether there is more than one God, it's very similar. Atheists use this tactic backwards and do not believe a God exists and try answering these questions by using scientific knowledge and facts.

The argument does not boil down to whether there is a heaven or not, it just boils down to whether the right morals are promoted. Help your neighbor and do what is honestly right for this world. Always avoid violence or fighting because too many people will be left hurt in the process. I believe that if there was a God out there that being would give us the freedom to make our own decisions and would promote what is in fact right in the eyes of the masses (positive energy). Jesus Christ was a great individual not because he claimed to be the Son of God but because he promoted the right message of peace, freedom, and sharing.

In my opinion, he's the one name that anywhere in the world most will know who you are talking about because he had such a significant impact on this planet—more so than most individuals known to exist (whether people think of this as positive or negative). The reason for this is he did what he believed was right and then died because of it, which he accepted.

Why his name was carried so far after death was because people came to realize what he stood for and believed that he promoted the right message. Forgive and forget, move forward, helping each other along the way. Promote the good in humanity. Increase the peace.

We will always be stuck on the question of whether there is fate or free will, so the answer is to edict your future so you will manipulate the results you would like to see in yourself. How? Through the choices you make, day in and day out. It's the habitual small things that turn into big leaps. It's the patience, the months, years, and hours put in to perfect something that will lead to whether you live the life you want. Not being average but rather working four times harder than everyone around you. In the end it doesn't matter how much talent an individual has because if you out work them you will be the last one standing. As I have said, we will all be stuck on this question of existence so just ask yourself this:

People ask the question why we die, when we cannot even answer the question of why we live and exist. Or if we created god who created us?

Even in your darkest hour, don't stop believing in yourself; keep the momentum moving forward. Like how Nike promotes "Just do it", well, JUST DO IT, even if you're complaining. This book is not meant to make people quit; it's about perseverance and overcoming adversity through struggle (mental and physical). Beating the pain that life throws at you. Concentrating on the inferior things never works out. It's like a huge stop sign.

Keep your brain occupied and busy so that you do not need to think as much (reading is great to keep the brain occupied). For example, if you are doing a cardio workout and someone is screaming in your ear, or if you are helping someone do something, it will act as a distraction device. The same reality applies to life, so get focused. Imagine yourself falling off a cliff and how you would have to concentrate to pull yourself back onto solid ground. You wouldn't be thinking about what you are doing tomorrow. All you would be thinking about is survival. Imagine yourself in survival mode every day. That if you don't do your best something bad is going to happen. The more you begin to focus, the clearer things become and the more opportunities you will see.

Keeping the mind occupied in times of despair is the best thing to do, rather than sitting and dwelling on things. When you dwell on your problems, the brain turns into bacon and eggs. When you're focusing your time and energy on something else important it can work as a distraction device to keep you busy, making you think differently. Even if you don't have a goal set, it still will work in your favor because it keeps you occupied. This distraction device can help you tune out the negativity and concentrate on something worth your while, something more positive. Working out is a great distraction mechanism even if you don't want to, the hardest part is just getting to the gym. Even if you are mediocre that day at the gym, at least you made the attempt to go!

That's the key: get your mind off the negative thinking so progression can start and turn into positive thinking. Another useful piece of advice that inspired me was from Steve Jobs, who said, "If it were your last day on Earth, would you be doing what you are doing now?" Stay productive, don't just sit and mope around, do something about it. If you're not getting anywhere, find the problem and fix it so that you will keep progressing. Seek guidance from someone if you need to talk things through.

The only time you should ever stop considering moving forwards is when you're dead. Even then if you were productive enough in the ideas you were promoting, your strength will carry on as will your message be heard.

Chapter 6
Laziness should never be an option

Laziness is a weakness that should never be considered a factor towards why you were unable to do something or perform the way you wanted to. Not trying hard because you're lazy—wrong answer! Do not think for one minute that a young child working in a sweatshop would not give his soul to have a regular life and not waste it sitting on the couch. Less fortunate people would give anything they could to live in something better than their environment (in a not biased sense). Although some people think it is much easier for these unfortunate lives, I have to disagree when here in our developed world we at least have the freedom to come as we please.

Motivate yourself knowing what these individuals would do for what you have in front of you. For these individuals laziness is beyond doubt not an option because if they quit and give up someone who will get paid even less will replace them. Laziness is just another excuse for why a goal was not met or success was not possible.

If you only get a B- on a test because you're lazy, some revision needs to be done, as well as some reflection, by putting yourself in the shoes of these poor suffering children and thinking, "How can I better myself to have an impact these less fortunate lives?" Especially when we all know in our hearts that if these poor struggling families were given the same life we have they would make the most of it. Think to yourself, the right answer is when a person says, "I gave it everything I had and I still came out with a B-." At least with that last sentence, there were no excuses; you have tried your best and will have to live with the consequences. Whereas if you are lazy, there is no consequence, there is just failure instead of success. If you don't even try to jump that hurdle, how can anything you do be relevant? This can be applied to any scenario.

People laugh at minorities taking low paying jobs to make a living. For some it's a much better condition than what they were exposed to. It's understandable that some people live in worse situations than others, but we cannot use this as an excuse for why you are not making moves in a positive direction. Especially in a place of opportunity. I believe it is not a matter of circumstance that effects one's life, rather a decision. Some of the most successful people started from nothing and turned it into something huge. People like 50 Cent or any rappers raised on the streets. This goes back to the defense mechanisms people like to use. A lazy person is full of thousands of these excuses rather than just putting forth a little effort.

A real leader and champion is not built from excuses; that person is built from their effort of never accepting "good enough" as an answer.

The comfort zone needs to be left aside if we ever expect to make a difference. Even if you are struggling, at least you're trying. If we don't leave our comfort zone, we will have an afterlife filled with regrets and "should haves, could haves, and would haves" rather than "I did this, I did that."

The point is, you feel better when you do more. When you are contributing, it feels great! Sitting there contemplating doesn't cut it. All it takes is for you to get up and do it. Don't make an excuse about why you are unable to do something, just do it or at least try—it's simple. If you do not at least try, how can you ever know if you are capable of doing something? Do you think in the past any odds were defied by being lazy? Definitely not, because the production would be at a halt and no profit margin would be met. My motivation is just thinking about how if I work hard I will have money and the skills to help people in need. I will not have to rely on anyone and will be self-efficient to help people be more positive in their lives, while at the same time promoting change. In doing this, helping others do the same.

Work has to be done in order for our world and it's people to move forward and interpret knowledge. Do you think soldiers of war can be lazy? If they are, say good-bye to everything they have earned up to that point in their life. Quitting in the real world leads to game over. That's it.

No more life or success. We as people have to want to give more than our bodies can take to make this ideal, this difference in the lives of our brothers and sisters. Honestly, be the most enthusiastic person at all times.

Lead by example, show people that you are not just blowing air—you are significantly trying to make a difference. Preaching and doing nothing about it will not help the situation. The point being, don't be lazy my friends. Just do something positive! I have never obtained a more positive high in my life than doing as much as I possibly can by helping others.

Get high off natural energy, at the same time motivating and influencing others. If people look at you differently, it's because they can't handle your energy and confidence. Don't fret—this is a good thing as you're the captain of your ship.

Even when you want to give up and die, DON'T. Keep pushing forward, telling yourself that it is all going to work out in the end. Take it one day at a time. It will pay off in the future by making you a stronger person. It will make the hard things in life seem easy because you have been there before and know you are stronger than that.

You're a soft, caring person on the outside but hard on the inside. You don't want to be known as a quitter or weak, do you? It sounds much better knowing you will be able to accept any challenge, even if you know you may not succeed. This will demonstrate the type of person you are, what you're true colors are. It's all about just attempting new things to help you gain experience.

The reality is, I cannot complain about my situation if I do nothing to change it.

There will always be times in life where you will feel weak and hopeless, but this is where that "show no weakness" attitude can benefit you. It will push you to places you never thought of because you are not giving into your mind wants. Rather, you are breaking mental barriers. This doesn't mean you should be hard-core, it just means that you will be able to handle things differently and more efficiently than others because you will not let things bother you as easily.

People will catch wind of this and, hopefully, start living by the same principles. Project that "I can do anything" attitude, with a smile always on your face and a positive outlook on life, trying to help others succeed.

Never give up on what you stand for, instead always laugh in the face of a challenge, never doubting yourself.

You're creating your reality. Rather than climbing the ladder, you're holding it down.

Weakness can make you vulnerable and become your worst enemy. Don't let this stop you from doing something, even if you are scared to change because you think you're too weak—you can always enhance knowledge. We as people know we are able to change. Some are scared to change, therefore change isn't possible. The other issue is most people fear being judged by others. The fact is that your mind will play tricks on you, so do the opposite of what it wants. Your physical actions will help change the way your mind reacts. This can work both ways. Your mind can make your body do something it does not want to. For example, if you are scared of heights or rollercoasters, get in line and go, or close your eyes and jump. Let your body do the work and your mind will follow.

When I was sixteen, I had a demonstration fight in Muay Thai in Cambridge, Ontario. I drove down and it turned out I didn't have an opponent. The trainer from that gym told me that he had someone for me but he was really tough and around twenty-three years old. I accepted the fight without thinking because I didn't want to look afraid. So here I am, warming up for the fight, thinking I'm going to fight this younger kid. Anyways, I remember kicking pads and looking across the room at this six-foot-two jacked guy thinking, "Wow. I wonder who's fighting that guy." So my name gets called over the microphone and I walk in behind my trainer and look up in the ring and it was that big, jacked guy.

It was a funny scenario because in a fight you can't just turn around; once your name is called there's no turning back. It turns out the guy's technique wasn't the best, so I picked him apart and left him battered and bruised by the end of the fight. What this goes to show you is that sometimes things will deceive you until you get in there and experience them for yourself.

Do you think Napoleon Bonaparte (famous general during the French Revolution, renowned as one of the best leaders in world history) would be as well known as he is today if he showed weakness, even when it was almost impossible for him to accomplish certain tasks? He was known for showing no weakness, even in the face of a struggle, which made him stronger as a person. He would sit in the middle of the battlefield with his troops where he could get severely injured or killed, never backing down. This is what made him successful.

For example, in poker if you have "a tell", this can be your weakness and more experienced players may be a few steps ahead of you because of this. They have no signs of weakness, which makes them harder to figure out and break. Always remember, when you have fear, it will make you think twice. Fear is only negative when it stops you from doing something. On the other hand, it can heighten your senses and make you more aware in turns being able to strike with precision.

Just learn how to control this fear so it doesn't interfere with your life. How? Challenge yourself by doing the things you don't like to do. Whatever you fear, make an attempt and face it—don't run away. This will help solve many obstacles within your life and help you better understand yourself. The more you begin to do thing's the easier they will become. The fact is that this fear may never go away but instead you will be able to handle it more effectively than before. No where am I suggesting you punch a bully or threaten that person, but imagine how they would feel if you did. What I am encouraging is for you to be yourself, to speak your mind, not worrying about judgment. I have a hard time with this when it comes to MMA fighting because it's dangerous, although I know deep down inside I will be fine, but there is always a potential risk. So in terms of risk management, I measure the benefits over the risks. Other than this, I will always try something new. That's what we are here to do, try new things. If you are shy, start voicing your opinion—it can't hurt. What do you have to lose? Project this image and it will become you. Don't let laziness define you.

Do you want to regret, or forget your fear? - Connor LaRocque
Don't fear a man if he bleed too. – Jadakiss

Chapter 7
Encourage people, don't discourage them

Encouragement is a big key to success and is indeed the answer to most situations in which someone wants to quit or give up on themselves. It's never a good idea to bring someone else down to make yourself look better. In your head, you have your goals and beliefs; if you honestly believe in them, no person should be able to stop you or bring you down because you have certainty in yourself. Let your confidence guide you. This is why encouragement is so important. With this tool, you can enable yourself to help encourage others so that they are able to complete their goals and desires rather than making them turn the page on you.

Giving encouragement will make you a team player and help you feel better about yourself. If someone doesn't like the encouragement you offer, that doesn't matter. You are who you are, trying to help everyone you can move forward. This obviously doesn't mean to criticize people because this can drive people to think you're better than them.

Make sure you let people know that this is not the case. You are just promoting the good you see in everybody, not the bad. Once people come to terms that your encouragement pushed them to limits they thought were impossible, they will remember your name and what you stand for.

For example, if you work out by yourself you cannot get as hard a push as you would if you have a trainer or someone watching you. If one of your idols was watching you, I'm sure you would try and show them what you're made of, as opposed to if you were working out alone in your basement. Constructive criticism is never a negative thing unless you keep running into the same problems without solutions. Ask yourself the right questions and you will receive the answer you want to hear. Don't become frustrated, become more focused. Criticism is good to help someone fix their mistakes so they do not make them again.

Reinforce people by telling them that at least they're trying and putting forth an effort. If the person is trying to push you away, then lay off and remember that at least you offered some support. Take the advice and give it, but don't go around trying to be Socrates (famous philosopher) questioning what everyone is doing, or else people may think you're a narcissist.

When arguments get heated and victory is near impossible, we as humans tend to go for the low blows to hurt other people's feelings because we feel that there is no other way to get a point across. Although the other person is winning the argument, you persist to take a piece out of your opponent to get recognition. In many political campaigns, you see this all the time, where a candidate is struggling to get viewers' attention so they bring up a family issue or lifestyle issue to get the audience off the positive delivery and onto the negative one. If you want to win an argument, have your bullets ready to deliver a concise, valid, and sound argument that will hit home.

The key point is to know when to attack and be prepared so that you leave your opponent pondering. If you have no inkling what you're talking about, save yourself the trouble and don't throw in your two cents. I had to learn this the hard way by getting a fist driven into my mouth, rather than just zipping it. Mr. Perfect is not always right.

Only attack during an argument when it's necessary, if someone is attacking you and you know you can contradict them. Other than that, don't even waste your time. What's the point of getting into a heated debate? If you get disrespected, be the bigger person and don't pull a low blow like your opponent is trying to do.

Use your tools of intellect to form a more concise argument that will hit harder than a low blow. It will take your opponent out mentally. Arguing everything is also not the best idea (although it's fun). There will always be a time and place to get into an argument and the dinner table, or in public, is not usually one of them. If you like to spend your time arguing I would recommend a debate team so you can put that time and energy to the test. Or write an article to vocalize your opinion. Or like what me and my friend Adam do: we voice our opinions to each other and go back and forth with the knowledge we know. Use your different points of reference to drive forth a thought-provoking argument. It will help you practice to acquire better negotiating skills. With this, it will offer different ideas and perceptions than your own.

I was once told to think of 250 people you know and wonder to yourself, "Do they think positively or negative about me?" If you get a lot of negatives, maybe it's time for some insight and change. If you don't believe so, keep doing what you are doing! Spend your time enhancing your knowledge and studying the mind so that when the time comes you will be able to quickly drop your opponent in an argument. Ask yourself, "Am I being too critical or just trying to help?"

Be ready to go 24 hours a day. There is never a time that you will give in or lose; you are a winner and a steady dreamer.

Chapter 8
Decision making is the ultimate power

We as humans possess the power to make rational decisions. This is something that money cannot buy. This vital tool will enable you to either give up or keep moving forward. Remember, as I said at the beginning of this book, not making a decision is in fact making a decision not to act upon something. Always remember, even though you think no one is listening to your ideas or opinions, they will grasp something from you. If you try to force a point or opinion, people will zone out on you because they don't want to hear what you have to say. Too many times in my life have I tried shoving my opinion down someone's throat or interrupting them when this is not the best way to get a point across.

I have tried to make things happen at an accelerated pace because of a low patience level when really, if you just let it happen with time it will come. My whole life has been about trying to making it happen. This doesn't mean that you stop working to achieve your goal; it just means you work harder so that it will happen. In doing this you will build a self-sustaining platform for future achievement and accumulation of whatever you desire. You will be creating a page in history by taking that thought from your conscious mind, then witnessing it with your own eyes. Don't sleep until you achieve your goal. The same idea goes for success; it will not just come overnight. People have to work hard by setting goals and achieving them. Like a knockout in an MMA match, if you try to make it happen and that's all that's on your brain, it more than likely will not happen if you are using your aggression rather than making the proper calculations.

In doing this, you will forget about what your opponent is trying to do rather than what you're trying to implement and just attack obliviously leaving yourself vulnerable. The same idea applies to life; if you try force an opinion or idea on someone too quickly, you can just as easily scare them off for good. Use these three basic tools that will be used throughout this entire book with the underlying premise, never panic and always stay: 1) calm, 2) cool, and 3) collected. In doing this you will logistically be able to react appropriately to the situation you are involved in. Even if it's a tragic event, it will help you keep your emotions in check.

The sun will always set in the west, meaning if you do not stay calm, cool, and collected your emotions can break you down mentally and make that hope for another day impossible. Why? Because you are digging a deeper hole in the ground that you will be unable to dig yourself out of. The sad reality is that if people who commit suicide could only realize this, that if they waited until the next day, they may have a different perspective on what they are about to do. Or speaking with someone about their difficulties. Recognizing the clarity of what was about to happen that they did not see the day before.

My old history teacher told my class that when you're finished writing an essay, put it somewhere and do not look at it or even think about it for a day. Why is this? Because it will allow you a fresh start the next day when you may have not seen the mistakes you made before because you were too focused on getting it over and done with. This can work with any piece of information as long as you use your time efficiently and do not procrastinate. The thing with procrastination is it is a double negative. Why? Because it will cause you more stress in the end by cramming you to get the work done. New days equal new ideas. Keep working toward your dreams.

When making a decision, try to look at it from your own perspective and the way someone else might see it. Look at both sides of the coin.

Chapter 9
We are transformers of our own destiny

Don't let other people's opinions of you change who you truly are.

Don't let anyone take away from you who you really are. Do you think Marilyn Manson (death metal singer) cares for one minute what anyone thinks about him even though he is portraying a negative message? No, and that's why he is successful in what he promotes. He is who he truly wants to be and no one else.

Take for instance someone like Rosa Parks, who helped push a cultural movement forward, that African American people should be considered equal. Do you think she was affected by what people thought of her? No, this is why a movement was started to promote equality enabling African Americans to sit where they would like on the city bus. It was much more than just this in general. It was about equal rights!

Look at Steve O, the star from the hit series *Jackass*. He always wanted to be a stuntman and went through numerous obstacles to perfect his dreams of living the "sex, drugs, and rock 'n roll" life. He accomplished this, so be careful what you wish for!

One of the best quotations I've ever heard, which I paraphrased from Gandhi, was "what you think is what you are." Whether you want to be a hockey player or a dancer, work towards that goal—look for the point of entry. If it doesn't work, keep trying because who is to stand in your way of you doing something you are devoted to? No other person is you; you are who you are and this is what makes you special.

If you don't become something you aspire to then try and work in that field. If you can't be a hockey player, well then do a job that involves hockey. The same premise can be applied to anything.

We create our own destiny, so if something's your passion, who is to tell you it's not? In the end, people will respect you for the effort you have given, even if at times people think your ideas are stupid. Why work a job you despise for decent money when you can work doing a job you love?

There were times in my life when I was laughed at and people questioned my intelligence, but you can never let that bother you because they couldn't see who I really was. It ate at me to the point that I started believing it. The reality was it made me question myself and act how I thought others would want me to. They judged me before getting to know me. Many people saw the negative before they had seen that all I wanted to give was positive. I will never forget what one kid once called me in a philosophy class: "Respectable, contrary to his looks." That stuck with me because that person looked past the negativity and got to know who I actually was. He didn't judge a book by a cover. He read it and genuinely came to terms with the idea that there was more to me than just filler and garbage. It took until I flipped a switch in my mind and in doing so set a higher standard for myself.

Too many times have I jumped to conclusions about people to only find out later that they were great. I used to have parents do the same to me because of the way I dressed and used vulgarity in my language. I always liked hip-hop so I used to dress like a gangster or rapper. This is why I will always give my respect to someone because if I don't, I am no better than the people who have judged me. Who am I to judge someone without knowing them? You must genuinely get to know the person to make such assumptions because who knows, maybe the first time you met that person they were having a bad day. At the end of the day, it's better knowing you didn't jump to conclusions.

Always give respect to all in what you are doing and portraying so you will gain the respect back for your gratitude and not your bad attitude.

Respect is not taught in a book. Respect should always be given because if there is no respect, what do you have? A great deal of arrogance and distrust, which is no way to live. Respect is a huge component of life, it shows the type of person you are. When respect is given, it does not go unnoticed. Never worry about being disrespected—it's irrelevant to your life. Just ignore it by going back to your fundamentals (i.e. helping people).

You may think your professor is unintelligent, but did that person not have to go to school to acquire that position? You may think your parents are stupid, when logistically they have much more experience than you and only look out for the best in your life. They protect you so you do not make the wrong choices and get yourself into trouble.

Someone may be more successful than you, and you might be envious of them, but just remember they put in their time and came out with the results. Inevitably, they seized the opportunity. We have to respect our elders, parents, teachers, trainers, and lovers for what they give to this Earth.

In my opinion, disrespect is just a sign of weakness. The same goes for jealousy because a jealous person just wants what you have earned. Too many times in school I have seen a teacher get disrespected for nothing and it really bothered me because it wasn't right. That person was given a job and a task to perform and doesn't deserve for that job to be made harder by a bunch of ignorant students. Like former President George W. Bush receives backlash about what he's accomplished when the man has a degree from Harvard University. Although this is a point for another time it goes to show you money can buy you better education.

People can say what they want about his father getting him in office to finish his job, but the man deserves respect. He was the President of the United States, one of the strongest countries in the world. He paid his time and was rewarded, no one can take that away from him (look up US presidents' ancestry—this will give you an interesting thought).

My point is to give respect to every human on this Earth. If you get disrespected, who cares? You know you gave your respect. The people you gave your respect to will remember this and hopefully will never forget it. For the people who were disrespectful, they will figure it out when they run into the wrong person. What goes around comes around, so keep encouraging, my friends.

"If you can't control your emotions, how can you ever expect to control your reality."

Chapter 10
Mindset is everything

Think outside the box so than you will appreciate your creativity and this will become your reality.

In my eyes mindset is everything. We cannot promote change with a negative mindset. Let me ask you something, if you knew you were going in for a life threatening surgery would you want a doctor who is the best in the business, or someone who is "good enough." With that in mind you now see my point—this is why you need to strive to be the greatest because if you are just mediocre at what you are doing, this will lead to mediocre results. The good things in life will not just come from the sky. In order to acquire the proper mindset, one must use mental cues to develop the right internal stimuli. To give you motivation just as music would being it is external stimuli. You need to think about yourself succeeding, being the best, and helping the most amount of people. Think about yourself beating your past records and how good this will feel to get recognition for the things you accomplish. Not the selfish things but rather the positive helping things. This is why I want to talk about plagiarism and coming into your own, with this your ideal unstoppable mindset. We all know stealing someone else's work is never a good option. On the other hand, you can learn from other people's work and then base your own thoughts off their ideas. This doesn't mean steal or use parts of other people's ideas, it just means come up with your own, possibly better, ideas. With originality, you're not just sticking to the same old script. Instead, you are bringing something unfamiliar to the table that may possibly revolutionize and enlighten the way people think, therefore springing forth new ideas. This is why it is crucial to be yourself.

People love originality because it can make you think differently and offer a new perspective that people can use to acquire a higher ground of knowledge. Throughout history, if people were not creating new ideas, do you think they would have gotten anywhere? Absolutely not—it's the free thinkers that bring forth new knowledge that can put a spin on reality, making things more efficient and easier to use and build.

The microwave and the computer brought forth a significant impact on culture and society. Cell phones even created exponential innovation, growth, and potential for a new epoch in society. If we were to use the same old jokes over and over, they would no longer be appealing and become boring. They would not gain attention. When new jokes are told, they grab people's attention because they are unfamiliar. This is what being original all is about: grabbing attention so that growth can happen. Think about this for a second—the government is supposed to create jobs when it is truly the entrepreneur who creates jobs. It is due to their originality that new jobs are created. This leads to my next quote:

"Do not be a text book definition – be someone who writes the text book."

What I mean by this is, don't pull all your facts from a textbook. You are capable of perceiving your own thoughts and ideas. Numerous times in my university classes, I have seen students doing this rather than putting their own twist on an idea. What do con artists get? Nothing. What does stealing someone else's ideas get us? NOTHING. Maybe money or a higher grade, but always remember it can backfire and get you sued or kicked out of school. If we the people ever plan to make a significant difference, originality is a shot in the right direction. Would you rather someone repeating the same old information or present something new and innovative? I think nine out of ten people would like to see something new, something different that is foreign to them, not just the same old corn on the cob.

The same rules can be applied to a legal system and its originality. Instead of using the same old common law, enacting bills and statutes, we could try something new that could possibly enhance the system— one that would not criminalize people who don't belong in the criminal system, but instead using our taxes on areas that need funding, rather than busting pot-head stoners. Unless they're driving under the influence, it's their life to waste.

I believe we should have a system that makes our criminals work rather than sit and build up anger in a jail cell. They should have to fix roads or pick up garbage. Pay their debt back to society so maybe they learn something valuable rather than learning negative techniques from other criminals.

Maybe this would make potential criminals think differently before committing a crime. If they go to jail they are going to have to do all the jobs everyday citizens don't want to (not getting paid for it, rather "paying for it"). If they break the law, they could be picking up garbage. Although done to some extent in Canada, this is not unfair, it is reasonable. In my opinion, this ought to be done to restore justice to society.

Originality is the start of great thought. Use it to your advantage and have faith in your ideas.

Chapter 11
Prepare to take hits on the battlefield called life

A useful formula to prepare yourself for anything is to plan your attacks and anticipate other people's attacks. How do you manipulate other people's attacks? Through watching everything they do and the way they speak. Doing this will reflect how someone thinks and will allow you to get inside their head. You can figure out what someone is thinking by letting them speak. Make sure you keep running your plans through your head so you will have perfected them. If you want to better understand and read people, watch the way they react to different situations. Whatever you are doing, visualize the goal in front of you within your mind, play that scenario over and over.

Review how you're going to react to the different scenarios that may get thrown in front of you, so that when the time comes you will be familiar with what is about to happen because you will have already been there in your head. Practice makes perfect. You will be able to strike with precision.

If you have a meeting, play it through your head one hundred times and have your thoughts ready to go. When the time comes to strike, you will be ready to drop your ideas clearly and concisely. There's nothing wrong with being over-prepared; it's when people are under-prepared that you may run into some issues. If you do not study for a test, how you can be angry if your results reflect this? It's the difference between having studied and getting good results because you were prepared.

Take for instance how well John. F. Kennedy delivered his speeches to the people of his nation. It's evident that he had perfected them. Even if you believe you have an easy task ahead of you, you still should have yourself ready to go. An old MMA trainer used to tell me that the truth comes out in the ring, meaning when you go in there, people will get to see if you trained or if you were being lazy and mediocre. The same premise can be applied to life because if someone is prepared and you are not they will be able to pick you apart. But if you are prepared then you will be on level playing ground and be able to compete at your full potential.

When you know someone is very skillful, outwork that person. Thinking from the top of your head and improvising can only work for so long until it will catch up with you. Never rely on the "winging it" tactic. Do you think if an army went in unprepared they would succeed compared to one that was fully equipped and trained? I don't think so. I'm absolutely certain the unprepared army would get annihilated. The reason armies like that of the United States are so successful is because they are prepared for any scenario thrown at them. The same goes for the North Korean army guarding their peninsula; some historians would argue they could beat the United States if they fought on their own terms in North Korea.

Another point I wanted to mention, which I learned from someone, is about neurolinguistic programming. This can help with reading people. This is done by asking certain questions to see if an individual runs on an internal or external drive. There are various questions, for example: Why do you not steal? Someone running on an internal drive will say, "Because I don't need to or because I don't like to." Whereas, someone running on an external drive will say something like, "Because I am told not to, or because society tells me it's wrong." These are good techniques to use to help understand people. Think up your own questions to add to your arsenal. I was taught more in-depth about this through one of my father's friends, who is keen in the field of conflict resolution.

Another useful tool is to find the right role model because this allows us to invent ourselves—it gives us inspiration so that we can one day aspire to be something like that person. Even if you are mimicking some of this role model's moves, it allows you to perfect your own. You need to learn from the giants if you want to be considered one of the best.

Obviously, don't copy them in every way, just use some of their moves to awaken your own creativity. Make sure you pick a positive influence as a role model; someone who promotes change, not someone who is pessimistic and always negative who promotes the wrong virtues.

Hollywood stars sometimes are not ideal because when you get to see them for who they really are it may shock you (although not all of them). I had to find this out the hard way by buying into all their weak-mindedness and vanity.

We have to remember these are people just like ourselves. They go to the bathroom just like everybody else. It's an interesting thought that hypothetically we idolize actors and actresses who are practically liars. What I mean by this is that all they do is act in front of a camera, yet we fall in love with these people because they play fictional characters we enjoy. This is just an interesting thought as they are not going to war and dying on the battlefield, for example. War veterans die every day yet we place more value when an important celebrity dies, in a sense.

Pick people who are charismatic, full of life and energy, motivated to help others and not just themselves. I look for people with the right mindsets because to me mindset is everything. I've personally been influenced by the revolutionaries throughout history, the ones who like to promote change. People like Tony Robbins, Darren Hardy, Henry Ford, Samuel Adams, Thomas Jefferson, Thomas Edison, Napoleon Bonaparte, Theodore Roosevelt, Napoleon Hill, Fidel Castro, John Kennedy, Pierre Trudeau, Niccolo Machiavelli, Rosa Parks, Laura Secord, Mother Teresa, Hillary Clinton, Oprah Winfrey, Anne Frank, Andrew Carnegie, Dale Carnegie, Jim Rohn, Zig Ziglar, Abraham Lincoln, Mahatma Gandhi, Steve Jobs, Georges St. Pierre, Plato, and Jesus Christ (not for religious reasons but because of the message he convincingly portrayed).

Pick the people who are out for the prosperity of this planet and its people and not for their own self-gain. Stay away from people like Adolf Hitler, Joseph Stalin, King Louis XVI, Osama Bin Laden, and Sadam Hussein (if you are unfamiliar with some of these people look them up and you will see why they are atrocious role-models). They are people who disrupt the positive energy of the world.

The world would be a much better place without such negative people. Yes, maybe at the time some of the negative in these people seemed positive and the reality is, when people needed motivation, these were the people there to guide them.

The only thing that would have been great from Hitler was if he used his genius skills of manipulation to make people do great things not horrible ones. However, through positive role models, we as people will be able to create an ideal self, maybe one who is even more influential than the last. There is nothing wrong with trying to be great. Being a nice, loving, and caring individual never hurt anybody. Drive yourself to be a role model who influences others. You never know who is watching you.

Chapter 12
Fear Nothing

I always remember what Mr. Miyagi said in the movie *Karate Kid*: "It is okay to lose to your opponent, just do not lose to fear." So in real terms, it's okay if life breaks you down and beats you up, just do not be scared to get back up and keep pushing forward. With this, challenge yourself where fear is present in your life.

Fear is just a state of mind. In order to overcome fear, you must face it. Be brave. Don't let fear of doing something to stop you from reaching your goal. Facing fear becomes easier the more you do it. Would you rather look back in the future knowing you did something you were scared of, or instead didn't do something you were afraid of? Like not talking to a girl or guy you wanted to because you were scared about what they would say, or saying something you feel. Fear has affected every human to walk this planet, since day one. It is the one emotion that effects every decision in our lives.

Once you overcome this fear, you will get to see a different light on this world because you are not scared anymore; in a way you are free.

Yes, it may be uncomfortable overcoming this, but in the end your future self is going to thank you. Start by taking baby steps; small things will eventually turn into bigger leaps. This may take time but eventually you will challenge yourself with anything.

Give yourself recognition for being courageous rather than being a coward. It's been said before: face your problems, don't hide from them. I still struggle at times in Muay Thai with what my trainer told me, "to attack my fears head on," but it's what has to be done to overcome this fear of approaching something.

This doesn't mean run, but in the right environment, walk forward into whatever you fear. We as people know it's hard to overcome fear but people do it every day. They get up on stage and perform, they put themselves were they don't want to be. Everyone is capable of doing it. Just start small and work your way up from there. No one can completely change overnight, but the fact is they can make a change in the right direction so that in time it will be accomplished.

The past may be there to haunt you, but as long as you are making changes, this will not last. The great thing about life is that we can change and when people look at you can say, "That was the old me." Control your future, don't live in the past. The same idea goes for fear. Take it head on and face your fear (change), or hide in the shadows (live in the past).

What do you think would feel better, facing your fear or letting it consume you and make you hide? To get rid of that fear that was always in the back of your head would be quite relieving, giving you satisfaction.

The great thing about this world is we have a choice to do something (although limited in some countries). You have the choice to say that you're not going to sit and watch people die, rather you are going to help them.

If you were in a position of struggling and suffering, would you not want someone to help you, to save you if you were going to die? Not to say this is the end, but rather, this is a new beginning for someone.

The unique thing about this world is that people can start from the bottom and work their way to the top. Start from nothing and turn it into something. Isn't this great? We can prove ourselves to the people who didn't think this is possible. This gives you credibility and leverage. It's great motivation to show that we as humans can overcome obstacles by staying positive, believing in ourselves, and working hard to achieve our goals.

Just think it in your mind, for example, how you perceive a thought when you're reading something. Just says the words "I believe" out loud and your brain will think it. You only think one thing at a time, no matter how often that thought is changing. It may be harder said than done, but people become successful everyday proving they can exceed expectations. People need to be shown how it is done so they can learn from this. If we never went to the moon, people would believe it impossible. Well, the reality is that nothing is impossible; it is just a word and excuse for why we are unable to do something or at least attempt.

Why can't you live a satisfying life making some of your dreams a reality? Who is to tell you you're not capable of doing something? Do not dread the mountain you have to climb, embrace it and get pumped up about it knowing you're going to make it. Enjoy the ride of life and be ready for whatever it has to offer without having doubts in what you can accomplish. Doubt leads to failure. In the book *The Secret*, the premise is to think positive.

Negative thinking never helped anybody. How can you expect to be released from your cage if you think negatively toward everyone or think everyone's stupid? Being positive is great encouragement not only for yourself but the people around you. Even if it is false hope and you are not able to succeed, it's much better than hearing "I can't." All I care about is if you at least make and effort and attempt to do something.

Miracles are real and you can feel the energy when they are present. On a family vacation six years ago, I watched my Opa die in in front of my eyes. He was seventy-four years old and climbed five flights of stairs in eighty degrees Florida weather. I heard a little tick outside our hotel room while my mom was in the shower and my brother and father were in the bedroom. I was reading a magazine at the time, and still to this day, I don't know what drove me to get up and open that door.

I got up and opened the door and there was my grandfather laying with his eyes in the back of his head, tongue out of his mouth, code-blue flat line. He had no pulse and here I was in complete shock, screaming for my father and mother to get over here. Instantly, my dad and brother began to do CPR while my mom was crying in a towel because her father was laying their dead.

I called 911 but was in such a state of shock my mom had to take over. I did not know what to do—I froze in a panic. My brother kept pumping, but finally gave up so my mom took over until she had given up as well. It was like a scene out of a movie. I could hear ambulances coming and people were all around us giving us their condolences for our loss.

In the midst of all this, the only one who never gave up was my dad. He kept doing CPR, not stopping until my Opa was alive again. The odd thing about this is the night before we were all laughing having drinks and my grandfather was making us all sandwiches. Anyway, my brother was crying, smashing his fist into a concrete wall, my mom balling her eyes out because she thinks that's it, and then the miracle happened—one of the best things I ever heard was my dad saying, "He's breathing." What a feeling of relief after everyone thought he was and gone coming up saying, "We're sorry for your loss." My father had done it; he never quit or gave up and had brought my grandfather back to life.

Once the ambulances came, my Opa had thought that he had merely passed out. That was not the case as he was dead and revived back to life. He even pissed himself in the process. Oddly enough, when the paramedics checked his vitals, they were all perfect and he didn't want to go to the hospital. After an episode like that, he was definitely going!

This was one of the craziest things I had ever seen and it took me years to come to terms that it was not merely CPR bringing him back to life. It was a miracle, something special and spectacular that is rarely seen. To this day, he is still doing great. They replaced a valve in his heart and he still laughs about it today. The amazing thing about the situation is that we all panicked—my mom, my brother and I. The only one who didn't was my father. He stayed calm, cool, and collected until the job was done, teaching me a valuable lesson: that anything is possible and can happen at any time. He didn't let fear and panic overcome him. He embraced the stress and found a solution. What this proves is he adapted to the change an embraced the fear.

Fear nothing that stands in your way to success; opinions are just words, not actions.

Fear is the one emotion we must control. We must take this negative fear and turn it into a positive obstacle that challenges us. There will always be fear, it doesn't matter who you are or where you are in this world, fear will be present at some point in time. The fear will either take over controlling you or you will use it as your motivation to find the courage to do something. If fear controls you, it will be hard to not live scared and enjoy your life to the fullest, worrying about every detail.

The people who do not worry about fear are guaranteed to live much more fulfilling lives because they will not be plagued with over thinking hanging over their shoulders. It will make you feel better as a person to just fight fear and get over it rather than letting it consume you. In a person's life, there should never be a time where we do not do something because we are scared to (in the right context).

This seems illogical but we must be willing to step up to the plate to stop letting fear dictate each and every one of our lives—once you beat it you will understand.

If a bully is threatening you, don't put up with it, tell someone because it's better than having to deal with it every day. There will be ways to get around it so you will not have to deal with a bully again. Or if you're having family issues, don't be scared to discuss them in private with someone. Even if that person warns you if you tell someone you are going to be in trouble. Do the logical thing.

Don't fear the consequences, laugh at them.

Certain people are able to use fear to scare other people into doing things. If you show people like this that you have no fear, it will be much harder to manipulate you and you will hopefully gain some respect in the process. In the right environment, do things that you will not regret like riding a rollercoaster. Or if you want to skydive, don't be scared—do it. You more than likely will not regret it.

I believe that not backing down from certain obstacles will help you discover yourself. Most people, I'm assuming, would rather be courageous, because it makes you feel better. Killing someone, getting into an unnecessary fight, or even stopping a gunman should never be an option. Some of these things can put your life at serious risk. Potential danger is different than fear. If you want to fight your fears, try to do it in a controlled environment.

If you want to fight, join a boxing gym; if you want to break your fear of heights, go skydiving or jumping off diving towers; and if you want to learn what to do against a gun, go do gun defense training. Go fire some rounds at a shooting range as well.

In order to control our fears and emotions, we must use the basic logic of either doing something, or not doing something. If you're scared of something either fight it or don't fight it—it's simple. Just remember we live in the safest living environment we have ever been in. Imagine thousands of years ago where every day it was either life or death. It's all about risk management.

Confidence leads to belief, which leads to success. Whereas, doubt leads to lack of belief which leads to failure.

Chapter 13
Don't base opinions on premature judgment

Facing judgment is one of the difficulties abstract to our first world. The only way to beat judgment is to learn how to use it as motivation. This is done by taking the negative an individual or group throws at you, and then looking at the positives in what you see you are doing. Nobody, and I mean nobody is perfect in this world. Maybe in a different realm of consciousness, but not within the physical material world. We all have faults, we all face difficulties, but one thing is for certain; no "one" is perfect. When someone judges you, let them. Just remember that at the end of the day if you truly believe in what you are promoting, what will it matters to anyone else who doesn't want to partake in your journey. Although there are some psychological disorders out their causing people to hate, to the most extent I believe everyone loves something. Even the mass murderers and killers have loved at some point in their lives. They may even like what they do, as sad as it is to say, but this is true. It's an extreme example but shows we all have love to give in a sense.

The sad reality is that some of these people, like Charles Manson, were put in some wrong situations, like getting molested at a young age, to send them off the deep end. At some point in his life, I'm sure he had love to give.

Look at Mike Tyson, one of the most feared boxers in the world, who is now such a peaceful guy. Look at the serial killer Ted Bundy, for instance, he was a sick man, murdering women, but when you look at the guy, he looks normal. Something in his life probably caused him to do such things or I could be wrong. The fact is that we cannot say that at some point in the man's life he didn't have a little bit of love. Even Hitler, one of the most terrible idiots to walk the planet, is said to have changed due to mustard gas, having syphilis or family factors (these are all theories; there are always other external factors). Although something must have been seriously wrong in Hitler's case.

I do not believe a person is ever born with hate (some psychological disorders may cause them to hate, but largely it's circumstances). Always remember some people have harder lives than others. I do not believe, like the philosopher John Locke, that our brain is merely a blank slate. I believe certain circumstances that someone is put into to cause such pain and anger. Some are able to cope while others dwell. We have natural instincts like animals but through our circumstances we develop. This is why some animals become domesticated.

It becomes evident that some people are able to use times of hardship as an edge to grasp and embrace the world in front of them. Whereas others it kick-starts a whole different world filled with hate and aggression. Some people are not as grateful to have a nice fulfilling life. Instead they are stuck in a life that someone would not want. This is why we WILL help and motivate people to escalate each other's another's attitudes.

Look at 50 Cent, who was raised in the projects and turned out to be a self-made success from the struggles he had to overcome. He had no father and mother died at 8, so he got stuck selling drugs during the crack epidemic. Others have a harder time dealing with things because they were not fortunate enough to possess the right tools to pull themselves out of the struggle.

That's why it becomes hard to judge people; we are all put in different situations with different external factors that can lead to different results. Force of habit causes people to assume things without getting the full picture. Our brain fills in the gaps. The only way to switch this is to be fully aware and ask the right questions to get a full understanding. In doing this, you give every single individual the benefit of the doubt. People all react differently causing a variety of different outcomes. Obviously, some people are stronger than others and it's good to use them as examples to give people motivation so that they understand it's all been done before.

A person has been there before so "I am going to be alright." The "never quitting" attitude never hurt anybody and, like I said, there will always be brighter days as long as we stay positive. If you don't, you may not have a fun ride and sink in the quicksand fast. Positive, Positive, Positive! Negative shouldn't even cross your mind. When you are always enthusiastic, how can someone disapprove of you even if it gets annoying? The way to break out of this judgmental sphere is to look at someone and tell yourself they are no different than you in that they are just living there life through there points of reference. Hence, they have desires just as yourself, meaning you should not judge them.

Would you rather walk the road to meritocracy or run the road to freedom?

Chapter 14
Equality should be a right not a privilege

Equality seems to be a constant struggle within this world. It's sad this idea that women are portrayed as inferior to men, in a sense because of physical strength and attributes. This is something I have yet to understand; it is a negligent concept that is bestowed within our realm known as society. Why I say this is because women bring to this Earth; the gift of life in itself. Without females, our world would be without existence.

It's reasonable to say that in our past, during the hunter-gatherer days, women took care of the children. But in the 21st century, this should not even be a thought, as women have proved that they are more than capable of doing exactly as men do.

Society as a whole has a cultural bias toward women (e.g. waitress and waiter) when the fact is we are all equal as people. Culturally, we oppressed women as we did slaves, when all we as people want is an equal chance to succeed and grow. This just goes to show the capacity of how greedy people can be treating others like material. It's just mind-boggling how throughout history, women were unable to vote and own land, or have the same rights as men.

The same goes for certain ethnicities. People wonder why there was so much animosity without any resolution. It was caused by all the oppression in our society, which is still happening in different parts of the world today. Why we as people cannot accept things as they should be is due to the fact that we are not on an equal playing ground.

The power establishment allows this to happen to increase security within their controlling realm and leaves the rest of us to deal with the issues with no solutions. Solutions include uniting together as people saying we are not going to stand for the imbalance anymore. If we were to take an anonymous test to show that people as a whole possess a general capacity to learn, it would not only prove that we should all be given equal rights, but also prove that what we are doing now is wrong.

Some of the greatest women to ever walk this Earth had to be oppressed to allow them to push movements towards equality: Oprah Winfrey, Anne Frank, Laura Secord, Rosa Parks, Mother Teresa, Joan of Arc, and Florence Nightingale, to name a few. There will always be competition—this is inevitable. It's just that we need an equal playing field, not only for women, but also for society as a whole. In doing this, we as people will understand our mistakes of the past and not only move society forward, but will be doing what is right. Looking from both angles, giving people an equal chance to succeed.

I never doubted that equal rights was the right direction. Most reforms, most problems are complicated. But to me there is nothing complicated about ordinary equality. - Alice Paul

The fact is the government only promotes this idea of equality and fairness to enable them to give people false hope and security. We can all think we are equal and try to become president or prime minister, but that doesn't mean it's going to happen. Someone can have all the fundamentals to be the greatest CEO of a company, yet someone else less qualified will get the position, why is that?

Chapter 15
Survival of the ego

It's time to break this egotistical mentality. It's time to put our egos aside for once and separate our differences. Looking at rules in general you either follow the rules or play by your own rules. Half of the people who create the rules break them when something does not go their way. They will not bend or break the rules when someone that doesn't matter to them needs help. For example, if someone who makes the rules gets into trouble they might try to bend the rules for themselves but not do the same for someone they think is irrelevant. This goes to show that half of the people who make the rules don't even understand their own rules.

In this world, if I follow by the rules I am given, everyone else should have to as well, especially if they were the ones who created them. There should be no ex facto law (veto power) to change something that is set in stone. In Canada, the rule of law states that all laws must be known in advance (accessible to the public).

Obviously, there will be room for revision but this should be after some act is solidified, not during the process. Meaning, we should only be able to change the rules once the game is over. So by law, no person should be punished if he followed the strict rules and guidelines he/she was given. Once revised for future cases and once people are aware, then they will be accountable.

We see rules being broken all the time, which is definitely unlawful. Only in very extreme cases such as genocide can we use ex facto law (veto power to enact whatever laws we want to). People acting like Hitler is another example.

The sad reality, in a sense, was that during Adolf Hitler's reign, people were playing by the rules. As awful as this sounds, it is true. They were going to "evacuate" the Jews, not exterminate them. What a loophole in a document. This goes to show the drastic extremes bending the rules can cause. This shouldn't have happened.

The people exterminating the Jewish people should have had the moral sense to know that what they were doing was wrong, even if Hitler's army was backing them, rather than this positivist approach to law. The reality is things like this shouldn't happen. This is why we as people must watch carefully to ensure we are not being lied to and that we are doing the right things in this world.

Everything goes back to this idea of equality and how as a whole, the world is not fair. I believe the reason that there have been so many issues in this world is because of inequality. If we level out the playing field within the world, we could achieve a movement. *"Stop the oppression, start the progression and end the animosity."* The truth is that the reason the world will continue to be unequal is due to the fact that parents will always look for their kids to get an uneven advantage. This could be done by means of paying for better schooling, or teaching them some fundamentals the schools don't teach them. Ultimately as much as we are all striving for excellence and trying to help one another, this will always be of concern. Obviously parents will want to see their children succeed first. That is just an interesting thought.

Why did Pontius Pilate kill Jesus? Because he did not like the type of change Jesus was promoting, which was a positive change. Over and over, people are getting shut down because of their ideas about helping others. It's an absolute joke. As mentioned at the beginning of this book, Mahatma Gandhi, John Kennedy, Martin Luther King Jr, Malcolm X, and Abraham Lincoln all promoted a message of change and were killed because of what they believed in.

The poverty gap seeks to perceive this reality as greed, which is a key factor in this. No one wants to face the reality that what they are doing is wrong. We would rather blame it on someone (or something) else so that we don't have to deal with someone else's problems—it's taking the easy way out. We spend millions of dollars on political campaigns and yet are not spending enough to benefit the poor in the long term. Initially with this idea of helping the poor we need to enable them to support themselves, not just provide handouts. Entitlement is a massive issue within North America alone. Some people truly need help, and we will always be there to help pick them back up, but it is obvious others can be doing more. Some people just don't care enough but this is going to change as more major issues start to surface. A man gave $50 million for Mitt Romney's Republican presidential campaign in the United States. Take, for example, environmental issues: gas prices and emissions are rising and water bottles are still being produced. In my hometown alone we have a garbage bin, recycling bin, and compost bin. The compost bin is not always used. We still see people throwing water bottles in garbage bins, which proves the point about how not enough effort is being exerted to make a change.

Obviously, people do care about the environment, but it's clear that not enough is being done because these issues are still escalating. No problem has yet to be solved, leaving us to think that a significant amount of people do not care. We still see significant amounts of waste, as well as people consuming more with no places to put all this filth. It seems it wouldn't matter how high the gas prices are, people will still persist to buy fuel. Too bad we couldn't just use all our garbage as gas to fuel our vehicles. Dreadfully, carbon emissions are increasing and resources are becoming scarcer.

Hopefully a drastic change will not come when it's too late, when we are unable to do nothing about it. The damages being done are because of the "procrastination effect" and will cease to prevail if the status quo is not met head on. As long as I can remember, it's been the same old song and dance. Minor adjustments have been made but more loopholes have been found to in fact keep doing what we are doing.

Ever since Al Gore's movie *An Inconvenient Truth* was released, I thought a drastic change was going to take place, but this did not happen. We still seem to be doing what we have been doing since 2006. Although recycling bins are used more frequently and there is a higher awareness for the environment, the garbage keeps piling up. We need to find a way around these environmental phenomena so we don't have to pay huge taxes in the future because once it really hits, then what do we do? Are we stuck being savages?

People can keep promoting change but what if no one buys into the change?

The fact is, the Green Party has no significant input because they do not have enough seats in the House of Commons to dictate; it's evident that not enough people are aware of the issues or want to prioritize the environment. New marketing needs to be instilled that is not just about government spending. This is where the major issues arise from—no one wants to pay money for the more expensive alternatives.

We need to figure out a way to make environmental initiatives cheaper and more convenient for people to produce, even if money has to be allocated to environmental programs to ensure the safety of our future generations. We need to help clean up the mess started from the industrial revolution.

The sad reality is, money makes the world go round.

How do we start this change? Through an efficient idea, backed with a mindset that says do or die. Innovate your thinking and grasp people's attention by doing something different, in doing this keep learning every day.

A thought for a potential solution would be stricter laws involving the environment. More cost effective environmental solutions that are not just about money. Something that is going to bring this movement off the ground, not just for the short term, but for the long term. There is no "if ands or buts" it has to be a MUST DO attitude!

Chapter 16
Darkness is the absence of light, so keep that smile shining bright

Don't let your shyness or quietness stop you from accomplishing something. If you really want to say something you feel but are scared to, say it anyway. Fight the urge that is stopping you and say it out loud, without regret. At first if you would like, say you are just kidding and see how that person reacts. Don't make it a habit! Than as you continue don't say anything at all besides what you want to. If you get judged because of it, big deal—that is your opinion and what you really believe, isn't it?
Don't let certain chances in life slip away, like asking someone out or being serious about an issue that is bothering you. I have said it before: be who you are. Be your true self and people will either like you for this or they won't. If someone doesn't like you, that person doesn't deserve to be in your life or even part of your time. Don't wonder through your life oblivious, rather pay attention to detail.

Go with your instinct if you feel it's the best option. Don't let the masses control your judgment. You are in control of your brain (although some people may try to get you to think otherwise).

A man who passed away once told me, "We are like cars; we must drive ourselves to our destination, but watch out along the way for bumps in the road." Obviously, don't be reckless or you can ruin your car (yourself). Be in control at all times and watch out for other drivers. Like driving a car, always watch out for other people's mistakes. They can hurt you in the process by taking you out of control.

If you feel a certain way about a person, it's not because of chance—it's because your body is reacting a certain way, either positive or negative (get to know them legitimately and maybe your opinion will change). Just be careful and don't be too naive. Be aware but at the same time, don't just listen to someone else's opinion of someone else, find out for yourself and then come to the proper judgment.

If you feel positive about a chance you're going into, take it—who knows, it could be the right decision. In doing this, it will alleviate some regret you may have in the future. If you feel negative about a decision, think twice about it and that could be the right decision (some people will deceive you by smiling in your face then backstabbing you). An old Muay Thai trainer once told me that with a risk there is a return. Always keep that in mind; be aware that some decisions you make can have consequences.

When you choose a behavior, you dictate the consequences. Remember if Barak Obama had not taken a chance he would not have become President. Even though he was African American, he beat the odds and is now running his second term as the United States President. This goes to show why we must take the right chances. Imagine what would have happened if Obama didn't run for office.

Roll the dice, take a chance—either way it's a win-win. You will gain experience, win or lose.

Chapter 17
You don't have to die to go to Heaven

Dreams are made when you realize the potential you possess to create change. The best dreams usually happen in everyday life. This world is your playground—look up at the sky or at the mountains and witness the true beauty of what you have in front of you. Life's a wonderful thing. Don't think that we only have so much time left, because time is an illusion. Realize this. My Grade 10 English teacher told me this and it's true in my opinion. Time goes faster when you want it to be slower, and vice versa.

If we didn't have life we wouldn't have anything; there would be no such thing as time because we created it. All time really is, is constant motion. Before the big bang theory, we had nothing. Let's define nothing: it's "no thing, not anything." What is it, then? Just pure white or darkness? Non-existent? We could play this game for hours and come to no significant answer. This is where the big bang can be questioned, if it started from this nothing and turned into something. This goes to show us that not everything is empirical.

Question everything and live in this great kingdom that is bestowed upon us. Enjoy every second you get to breathe oxygen into your lungs. Even for the less fortunate people who may not be able to hear or see, they still appreciate life. I have the utmost respect for these people and only wish they were able to see the world as I do—a no pain and suffering reality—just love, caring, and prosperity is all that matters.

If we just fight all the time, how can you expect to enjoy this beauty, while you're lying on a bloody destroyed battlefield? War should never be the answer as it gets us nowhere—it just leaves lives broken and destroyed having to rebuild the world we once had. Why should one have to die or give their life so that others can live happily?

We should rather enjoy it all together, helping one another every step of the way. Not blowing each other's heads off for a cause that is forever questioned. I personally believe that throughout history there could have been significant amounts of knowledge acquired by talking things out rather than having fights and killing one another.

Prize fighting should have been done to solve matters, something like the gladiators or extreme debate. At least then, some aggression could have been relieved rather than a massacre. Although everyone on this planet cannot agree on everything, there are indefinite things we can agree on: everyone wants personal security, food, water, shelter, and love. If people want to fight, why should it be to the death? Although conflict is inevitable, there are always logical ways to solve matters. In today's world, if you step back and look at society, negative actions are being portrayed such as greed, jealousy and lust, rather as caring, sharing and encouragement. This is about to change, because it has all started due to the power imbalance of this world. Why some people get rich and other's struggle is due to the type of mindset they have. This is what I truly believe. Although the facts do not lie that 85 people in the world have just as much as 3.6 million people. Is it just me or is there something wrong with that fact?

Chapter 18
There will always be doubts in life

Since we are in control of our lives, making the right choices is a valuable and vital thing. If you are having a bad day, it could make you think differently than you normally would, so be aware of the decisions you are making and the consequences that may follow. Step back and think, is this what I would want? Tomorrow, am I going to be happy with the decisions I made today?

Everyone wishes they could go back to a moment and relive it differently. This is why making the best decision possible is vital to ensuring you will have fewer regrets tomorrow or in the future. Don't make any decisions when you're really angry because it can throw you off, leaving you the next day to have to face the problems you started with the day before, except now you're not angry. It may seem like a good idea at the time to tell a parent, co-worker or teacher off, but in the long run, it can seriously affect you. Only make decisions that you absolutely feel good about. If not, then revise the idea and look for all the other possible outcomes. This is where being focused can help you. Why? Because it can enable you to react appropriately to any given situation. Take three deep breaths, slow the brain down and come to a decision. Just keep your mouth shut and wait on it.

There will always be bad days but on the bright side, a new day can help you create a new you, bettering yourself from the day before. You never have to live a life being the person you were, you can live a life becoming the person you want to be—the person you will be able to look at in the mirror and say, "I am happy with the decisions I have made." On a bad day I will just wait it out and see if I would make the same decision tomorrow.

The chemicals in the brain can play tricks on everyone, making us want to do different things than others. This is why we must try to learn to control our mental monologue so we are able to stay focused and in check at all times.

When you're angry, try to laugh it off. Avoid giving into what the brain wants. If you're sad, smile. It just takes minor changes to trick the brain and not give in to what it wants. Five deep breaths in and five deep breaths out. Slap those negative vibes from beneath you. Even when feeling tension or irritation, ignore it. Keep on with your day by staying busy so you do not have to think about it. It will subside, you just must be certain it will. Breathing can keep us calm, especially when not enough oxygen is going to the brain. Breathing enables us to think more clearly.

When adrenaline is pumping, we feel alive and react to certain situations differently. Use this adrenaline to your advantage, to give you an edge in helping you to think and react to things more clearly, to enhance your focus. Use the body-mind connection to help control the anger that's building up inside of you and try to work it out physically. Breathe and try to focus by controlling the way you think (i.e. think of how you're going to defeat your opponent).

Everyone has anger; it's the people who are unable to control it that are weak-minded, in my opinion. The person who cannot control his anger just has to believe they can control it and focus time and energy elsewhere to overcome it. Walk away when angry and go do something that makes you happy. Don't settle, work at stopping your anger at the source. Ask yourself, what is causing it? Than do what makes you feel good (not drugs, rather something like exercise). Drugs will just leave you lost and act as a temporary solution. I wouldn't even consider drugs a solution, rather an escalation of a problem that will later surface, making you face what is in front of you.

it. They build a bulletproof self-sustaining platform for the rest of their lives. How do you do this? Well, you figure out what you want to do and work toward it. Fail over and over, until you succeed. Temporary defeats are what mold you. You need to be educated on your subject on interest. Know as much as you possibly can, don't just study sometimes, be studying all the time. The problem with myself, which I don't consider it a problem is that I have programmed my brain to always be looking at what I can do next. I am completely restless and although this can be quite stressful it keeps me on my toes. It allows me to push myself when others are sleeping. It allows me to push myself when others are watching TV. It brings me satisfaction to know that I am giving it everything I can, and still can give more. It's like a champion prize fighter, they are willing to do what other average fighters are not. You're probably asking yourself how I have encoded this restless personality within my subconscious mind. First start by doing as much as you possibly can and it will become habitual. Utilize the internet or books that will enable you to better understand and grasp your desires. In doing this allowing you to perceive numerous angles on whatever it is you are trying to accomplish. I've found that with myself in general, when I am focused on a task at hand, when I can only see it being achieved, with no doubts being projected, then will I accomplish my goals. If you were to walk up to me right now and say I am going to become a millionaire by just going to school to become an engineer, doctor, lawyer, or accountant, I would laugh. Why? It wouldn't to be rude but rather because isn't this what everyone does expecting to get rich? Go to school like everyone else, and then expect the dream job to come out of nowhere. Well the fact is this is not how life works, especially in the digital age. This is why I am trying to drill home this idea of working after hours, studying more, volunteering more, pushing yourself to peaks you thought were impossible. Not following the metaphor that "you have all the time in the world" because you don't. If you choose not to be the best, you will not succeed to your full potential. I am not saying it is bad to become an engineer, lawyer, doctor, or accountant that is far from what I am implying. I am just saying if that is your passion, go be the best within that field. Push yourself to be the innovator, the revolutionary! This will not only make you credible, more

Chapter 19
The world can be a dark place, but it does not have to be

Realistically the world is in fact not fair. As we get older, we start to realize that there is a significant amount of pain and suffering in this world, more so than happiness and pleasure. We see people struggling to survive financially while others become wealthier, making the poverty gap forever widen. The 1% vs. the 99%. The number of wealthy is getting smaller yet the number living in poverty is getting bigger. What a paradox.

It's sad that in a world filled with such beauty that there has to be so much suffering and struggling, such negativity and doubt, that it causes people to fail and make them quit. While the people who don't have anything must take the little that they do have and make the best out of it, they must accept it.

Sometimes those who do achieve success laugh in the face of accomplishment only to say they have finally made it. The one question that has many answers is a puzzling one: Why do some people make it and why others do not? If you truly believe that you can cross the poverty line, will it actually happen? Can you make something out of nothing?

What does every successful human being on this planet have what others may not? They have the fundamentals in whatever they are doing: values, discipline, hard work, belief and perseverance; working harder than others, putting themselves at risk of failure, stepping outside the safe zone to cross those boundaries into the danger zone. The most important variable is that they love what they are doing and are passionate about income, and it will allow you to HELP MORE PEOPLE, which is what I am promoting.

Understand that some people are different, it may take tragedy for some individuals to become stronger, while for others it comes naturally—it flows in their blood. Some have that ability to adapt to whatever the circumstances may be. Other's need practice. You need to be able to take what you have and make it into something. If you do not work hard and dedicate yourself, how can you expect to be successful or even make it last? Why do you think so many people go bankrupt after hitting the jackpot? They stop working hard, they lose that fire that kept them burning. Perseverance dies along with their success. What do you have without belief? Nothing, blindness.

I genuinely believe that to be able to stay relevant in this millennium you must have a plan, work hard and not stop. In doing this seeing the future in advance. Act as if it was your first day on the job. Wake up in the morning knowing what you got yourself into and why you want to successful. Don't take the easy way out to get to the top instead of working at it and achieving this success you desire. These get rich quick schemes are nothing but false hope. They are so-called distractions to take your eye of the prize and the fact that true success comes from patience, hard work and a solid plan of action!

All that matters is if you work hard and if you feel like a success in your own eyes. It will help give others that work ethic when they see you grinding it out, day in and day out. Big deal if you don't get everything you wanted—you will come out with a better work ethic than most if you keep at what you're doing as well as the fact that giving it your best makes you feel better as a person. All that matters is if you are a success in your own eyes. Then you will be able to give back to the people who are left with nothing.

At the end of it all, would you rather know you worked hard and made an honest living, or do nothing and scrape by always saying, "I should have, could have, and would have"? Belief leads to confidence, which then leads to not quitting or giving up. The quitting factor is what hurts people. If you ever feel lost, ask yourself what makes you happy, what puts that smile on your face?

You must be willing to take that one extra step and not be afraid to get hurt on the battlefield; realize life hurts more if you shy away.

Chapter 20
Just breathe

What is the first thing we do without thought every second of every day? We breathe. Breathing is a necessary, basic essential of life. Without air, we would die. The last thing we do before we die is we take our last breath. The same goes for when we enter this Earth, we take a deep breath. Breathing is our start and our finish. When life becomes frustrating, rather than cluttering the mind with negativity, try deep breathing techniques to be able to help you relieve the frustration. It can put your pulse back to normal, not increase it.

Breathing can bring your energy level back to normal because breathing controls the heart rate. If you are breathing hard, the heart's beating faster, whereas if you're calm the heart rate is normal. If you are not able to breathe when things become complicated, how can you expect to think clearly when not enough oxygen is getting to your brain? The only way to focus clearly is to breathe; it's the best technique to help the body. This is what people do when they meditate—just focus on breathing in and out. Deep breaths in, deep breaths out.

Even if you have anger issues, this is the best answer, rather than slamming your fist into the wall or doing something that you might regret. What do you think is better, walking away and breathing during a heated argument, or getting more frustrated not being able to think and react as clearly in terns making you look incompetent? I think we all know the answer to this question. When the body is calm the brain can make precise calculations, whereas you can make the wrong ones when you're irritated and all over the place. When you're calm, you're able to think clearer and react better, without panicking.

What happens when you panic? You lose oxygen to the brain and lose focus to think clearly. The chemicals in the brain become unstable and out of balance, making the body react differently than if you were calm and collected.

Staying calm means you will be able to be in control at all times, rather than blacking out in rage. If you are in a drastic situation, like someone having a heart attack, it is much better to be calm rather than panicking and panting all over the place. How can you focus when you are all over the place? You can't.

If you become frustrated in situations where there is little time for error, staying calm could mean do or die. If you are able to stay calm when everyone else is not, you will be able to take control and make the proper judgment that someone panicking will not be able to make. The same premise applies if you are severely injured or someone around you is. If you are screaming because someone is bleeding, you will just make the situation worse, rather than calming the person down and making them feel safe.

Panicking can leave you vulnerable because it will take you away from the problem and make the brain focus on something else that may put you in shock. What happens if you were skydiving and your chute didn't open? I think your survival rate would be much higher if you stayed calm rather than scrambling all over the place. This may be difficult, but you must breathe and focus to let your body and mind react. Or if you have seconds to make the right decision, panicking will eat away at the time you have rather than you staying calm and thinking clearly. How you do this is to conceptually understand the situation you are in, take five deep breaths, and tell yourself everything is going to be alright.

Stay calm and at least you can hope that nothing will go wrong, but if you panic, you could leave yourself broken down and mentally stranded.

How this all ties together is that fear is a part of our everyday lives; it has haunted me since I was a little boy. I want you, the reader to challenge yourselves. I have come to realize that real happiness comes when we alleviate this fear of fear itself. When I was sad in life, it was a matter of bringing myself out of it. No other person was controlling my body. I was in control. This meant that when I was depressed about something, I had to snap out of it. No pill, no advice could bring me out of that state, I had to do it myself. The same goes for everybody else. You have to make a decision and stick to it. In doing this punishing yourself when you break away for the standard you set. Cognitively you must look at why you are acting or feeling the way you are, and then try looking at the different outlets that will enable you to break out of that mental state. Not why you have issues, but what the solutions are!

Although we are each different as humans, we all have the same basic emotions. We all feel the presence of life in front of us, allowing us to feel pain and battle our emotions. A world champion told me the basics of sports psychology revolve around three things: thoughts, emotions, and actions. When one of these comes out of place, we must use the other two to allow our bodies to react the way we want them to. To bring the third variable up to par with the other two.

The same goes for happiness. No drug is needed to have a euphoric feeling. Get high off life. Get high off reality and what sits in front of each and every one of us. If you are sad, bring yourself up by looking on the bright side of things that you are alive right now. Not that you're strapped for cash but that you're going to make more. Do not keep repeating the same cycles over that are you dragging you down. Break the habits that effect you negatively. Enlighten the way you think and allow your body to change according to the things that are thrown in front of you. Tell yourself what you want to hear and how you want to feel. Don't suppress your emotions—fight them using reverse psychology. One of my addictions in life is my hunger for knowledge and learning as much as I possibly can.

Once you master your attitude and have high confidence in your capabilities, nothing will stand in your way. No person will get in your head because that fear is gone. If anyone says I am too cocky, I just laugh, because the fact is I am just highly confident and believe in my capabilities. I just let my body react to certain circumstances, which enables me to be myself rather than over-think. Like UFC champion Jon Bones Jones says, "He puts his pants on in the morning as I do."

Initially, it becomes evident that this world is run by control and manipulation. If you let the fear get inside of your head, you will never get to experience the true reality of this Earth. The fact is that some people are living in wheelchairs struggling to get out of bed in the morning, while others work for a quarter a day in a factory and have absolutely nothing. Some people are even war veterans missing limbs.

This world of ours has set a stage for the have and have nots. If we just sit back and allow this to be our reality, we accept the fact that we either don't care or are weak and don't want to change. We allow ourselves to become part of the fundamental problem.

Just think for a second what we go to school for. Although off topic, this explains manipulation in a different sense. First of all, we go to school to be able to get a career to make money to support ourselves. Yet, what is the one thing they neglect to teach us in school? How to make money or even budget properly. They teach us that one day this dream job will just come out of nowhere if we go to school. Well the fact is, this is where the proper mindset comes into play. You need to do what you enjoy or else you will live the rest of your life making excuses towards why you aren't perfecting the reality you would enjoy to live in.

This is where if you follow the steps in this book and make yourself a plan of action, which will help you enhance your knowledge, you will become indestructible and motivated. Mark my words: do your research. People say they want money, well if you want it so bad, then why are you not doing anything to get it? Sacrificing sleep and leisure time. Taking any job to put that cold hard cash in your pocket. Just think about this for a minute. Why is the government not showing us other ways to make money? Because this is left to us the individuals to find the secrets. Not everything is handed over in this lifetime.

Remember, if you embrace the power of life, attacking problems head-on, realizing that others have much bigger obstacles to overcome than you do, only then will you come to realize the true potential and power of making a difference. Education is meant to teach students to think critically, yet everyone just accepts the fact that this is how life is meant to be. Control yourself, whether it pertains to drinking caffeine (drugs) every day, overeating, or being addicted to cigarettes (nicotine), it challenges each and every one of us.

Set yourself the proper standard to instill you have a guideline to work with, in doing this not accepting anything less. We must choose as people to create a positive attitude. An attitude that means we are not scared to do something and change. A positive perspective every day of our lives with no exception, no matter what the circumstances. In doing this, we will comprehend that we are not weak-minded. But for the rest who are stuck wanting to do something but are unable to, full potential is not met. Seek guidance if you must! Why I say this is because winners are made from their losses.

They are made from getting knocked down numerous times and not giving up by getting back up. Do you think Henry Ford invented the V8 engine in his first attempt? No, and while all of his people told him it was impossible, you know what he did? Made it happen. This eternal fire burns in every creature known to exist on this planet; you must just find a way to unlock this true potential and open your eyes to what is in front of you. Do the things you hate doing and tell yourself "this is awesome." It will only make you stronger.

The stars will align and you will know it's your time to shine.

Visualize what you want to happen, then make it happen! Set goals and achieve them. Absorb as much knowledge as you can from everyone around you—everyone has a story that can enable you to think differently. We are only on this planet for so long, so don't be scared to say or do something because it will all be gone in death.

If you are unable to comprehend something within your own subconscious realm of thought, how can you expect it to happen in the physical material world?

Better yourself every day and understand that we, as humans, are capable of the highest peaks. People have proved this before, but now it's your turn. Fear nothing.

If I get knocked down 50 times, I will get up 100.

Stay calm, breathe, and clear your mind. Now challenge yourself! What don't you want to do right now? Yes, right now, go do it. What's stopping you?

Chapter 21
My story

This is my story—what drives me, what guides me, and hopefully what I share will help you to relate as well as apply some of my experience to challenges you may be experiencing in your own life. You need to understand my life to see through my eyes.

With a positive outlook on life, you are indestructible—no one can stand in your way because your attitude will not let them.

As I have been stressing in the previous chapters, we must have high concentration and focus to be able to instill some of the things I have spoken about. To show how I came to my own conclusions, here's a look into my life.

From day one, since my cognitive reasoning was present, I always wondered to myself why people were struggling and starving while in my life I felt blessed. It didn't make sense why some people had things that others did not—why some kids in the schoolyard had better toys to play with than others. As a child, all I had was love. I didn't have a hateful bone in my body, and I would never get angry at anything. I was terrified of everything. I have always recognized the positive things in people while others were filled with such anger and hate. Since my mom was such a caring individual, she made me oblivious to the cruelty of the world in front of me. My brother would bully me every day when I was young and called me fat, driving my confidence to an all-time low. He instilled fear in me from a young age. I never understood why he would do this. When I would get made fun of or teased, I would accept it out of fear of what could happen if I stood up for myself. I was a scared kid in this huge world because of the fear that was around me. My lack of confidence affected me in a vast way because I didn't believe in myself, which left me to always look up to others. In doing this, I never gave myself credit.

I wouldn't be myself growing up because I always thought I had to be someone else. I worried about what others thought of me and it changed me as a person. I always felt stress and that in itself made me react differently. The thing with myself is I was always one to accept defeat. When my team would lose a competition, many would become upset, when I was able to handle things with ease, taking it as an experience.

I understood at a young age that you can absorb knowledge from anything. I may have always been positive, but I was negative toward myself and that affected the ways I dealt with issues. One of the greatest things that has ever stuck with me came from Steve Jobs. What he said was, *"Once we realize that everything around us was created from someone no smarter than you and I, then you will achieve your true potential and you can make a difference in the world"* (this is how I paraphrase what he said). Let things like this motivate you to want to make yourself better and try to create a bigger footprint than these people. Tony Robbins is a huge inspiration to me because of the simple yet essential things he promotes toward motivation. Some people think it's all common sense, yet they do not live by these principals.

I understood from a young age that it all boils down to choices in life—we choose to listen or don't. I was always a believer in fate, but the older I became the more I have come to realize we as people create our futures through our attitudes and driving forward with a concise goal, even if we fail. In my view of life, mindset is everything. The most valuable tool we as individuals possess is being able to learn to educate ourselves. If you are eager to gain knowledge because you recognize it's valuable to you, then you will see what others do not. We never stop obtaining new ideas and ways of thinking, so use this to your advantage.

Use this as a tool to allow yourself to think differently than the pack and utilize the time you have here on this planet. Don't be shy; get high off life and all the great things it has to offer. Just always remember at the end of the day that you can always do and give more from yourself. This is a fact, because even after I have pushed myself to my limits I still know I could have given more and taken one more step.

Every mind has its resistance point; you just have to discover that you can break it.

Ever since I was a young kid, playing sports was something that enabled me to grow as a person. I believe every kid should be able to get involved in something—it's one of the great motivators of life. I was raised a hockey player and through watching my brother terrorize everyone on the ice it made me envious. I wanted to be just like he was with no fear when faced with competition. These were the types of people I idolized. The fact was, I was not a fighter at that point and lacked the primal nature of it. I didn't have an intense edge that sometimes drives people to the peak of craziness. My brother did though—he had anger issues, as most enforcers in hockey do.

He is a well-liked guy, just short tempered, which made him a great grinder and fighter in hockey. I had what he didn't though—the heart and the discipline to listen to people. Where he would tell someone off, I would not. Or if he would fight someone on the ice, I would not out of fear. My coaches could see I was a great listener, eager to learn and that added a value that many players took for granted.

It was annoying growing up being overweight because it meant that the people who were faster judged me on my weight rather than my skill and personality. I was always such a nice kid to my teammates, but others would treat me with disrespect because I was fat. Hey, what can I say? I liked to eat.

Because of this disrespect, I used my brother as a crutch, talking about him because he had influenced me so much in my life. I had the belief that he was invincible. I thought no one would be able to stop him (maybe the law), and that caused me to tell everyone about him because I was impressed by him. He legitimately terrorized kids on the ice. He was my brother, but at the same time, he had his teammates make fun of me. Don't get the wrong idea, my brother is great, he just had some fun growing up.

They would call me names liked Condom and Confat. It was rough on me as all I wanted to do was feel like I belonged. Very few of his team members would accept me, and the ones who did were great guys. The one benefit to all this negative energy was the fact that it made me stronger as a person. I always knew one day I wouldn't be fat and would be able to progress my life in a positive direction, being mentally stronger than those who doubted me.

I had the awareness that, compared to my brother and his hockey mates, my thinking pattern was different. I was a much more caring person who looked for positive things in people. I would become so upset with the negative that it was a blow to my mental capability for some time. I did not think I had talent, and I didn't think I was smart and able to learn the same things that others could.

The reality is, it was all sitting there in front of me. I just had to go out there and prove to the people who laughed at me that they had misjudged me. I used to imagine if I was not fat how things would have played out. Things probably would have been the same except I would not have had the fat complex compounding things. In the end, I was ultimately happy. Even with the lack of confidence I possessed, oddly enough, I still didn't ever give into peer pressure.

This is a side point on conformity and peer pressure to show certain things I have learned. I can remember numerous times in my life when I either turned something down or just thought to myself, "This isn't the best idea." This allowed me to make some fundamental decisions in my life and separate myself from the crowd. Although I was never the best at saying "no" to people, I was somehow capable of not giving into peer pressure. Why I never gave in to peer pressure was because I understood the consequences. I realized that it could certainly affect me negatively in the future. I remember numerous times in my life when the people around me tried to get me to deal drugs because I was a bigger kid. I always said no because I didn't want to throw my life away.

As a child growing up, this is a major factor that influences everyone. What I came to terms with in myself is the fact that when we as humans understand something is not right, we must not be afraid to act on it and do the positive thing, which means not giving into peer pressure. Most people do not act because they are scared of being judged.

This is one major problem with our society: the idea of conformity. Kids today will rely on others to make their fundamental decisions and might possibly look to the "cooler kids" in the group to teach them the ropes of growing up. Individuals do this out of being scared of judgment. The problem with this is the younger generation is just setting themselves up for failure in the real world. I say this because if they listen to these "cool kids" and start smoking a cigarette, then it's obvious that these people will continue to follow some of these patterns and conform as they grow up. In turn they will not follow their dreams but instead live someone else's.

Let's be honest with ourselves now. How many people do you think actually enjoyed smoking at a young age, rather than just thinking it looked cool? I think we have an obvious answer here because the majority of the population now sees a major problem with it.

The power elite get students to subconsciously conform through the power of fear. It's like the example of "don't touch the iron because it's hot," except in a broader context. In order for students to make the right decisions in their lives, they have to be shown the true consequences of their actions. In doing this, understanding that their future could be jeopardized if they think it is all fun and games now, their perspective may greatly change in the future. School is not enough, it's the research you do after school is done for the day and what you do in your spare time that counts. The hours of planning before you strike. If you know something and do not apply it, it is useless to you. Texting and driving is going to be a major issue in the future. I can almost look at one out of ten cars and see someone texting.

We have to instill this same idea into the young that choices are everything, that we can never turn the clock back, and that we are able to create ourselves not out of fear but out of the way we feel. We must not be looked at differently because we do not conform to the status quo, but because we have a deeper understanding of what's going on around us. Lead by example.

Teach the young to always think twice about what is going on around them, to listen to their teachers and parents but at the same time know the difference between right and wrong. This is one of the most drastic and basic principles in a young person's life; understanding the power of decision making.

Don't just scare the young because eventually they will come to terms with this; instead prepare them for the long road ahead.

Bring your son or daughter to a crash site of someone who was texting and driving. Put that thought in their head so they will associate texting and driving as pain. Look at what television does to young schoolgirls—it makes them believe they have to be perfect, and that what happens on the television is in fact real. We live in a time when we are being fundamentally dictated to an extent, yet we do not realize what is going on in this world. For the people who do, most fear being judged. Why I say this is because we buy into all this vanity portrayed in the media, rather than using our fundamentals, which are helping one another grow and prosper. I don't watch television anymore because it is corrupt and in my opinion hurts our mental capacity as well as distracts us as people. One twenty minute show a week if I am lucky.

Dealing with the low confidence I had was hard. It meant I could never be who I actually was. I was always worried about being judged in the eyes of others. I was a random kid and I would say the stupidest things because I was nervous. I never spoke my mind because I hated it when people would laugh at me. It gave me an irritated feeling in my heart. Acting differently to avoid these laughs did nothing but create someone I was not. It actually made me look even more incompetent and flawed my communication skills.

The fact is, this is one of the biggest issues I see with our society, people being scared of being judged by someone. We are told how we are supposed to be and if we think otherwise, we are corrupt. In the right context, this doesn't make any sense to me. Something like gay people being judged for how they truly feel. Or, for example, an ethnicity not accepting a biased system of job hiring. If you do something out of the ordinary, people look at you differently. Some will follow you but some will think you are crazy. So please be yourselves and express how you feel. Like I said, seriously ask yourself, what is the worst thing that can happen? Who is this "someone" to be judging you in the first place? Remember some of the most successful innovators of thought were told their ideas had flaws and that they would never amount to anything. Yet we look at some of these people now and what enabled them to make their dream a reality was the certainty they had in their belief. They had seen what others had not, which allowed them to persevere. Some examples of people who did this are Mahatma Gandhi, Abraham Lincoln, Steve Jobs, Mother Theresa, and Hillary Clinton to name a few. The great thing about being different is you stand out more. In doing so you won't be looked at as average or generic.

Anyways, back to my story. In one hockey game I thought I would go out and recreate what my brother had done by hitting bodies all over the ice. Everyone loved it—it made my team love me until I hit a kid in the danger zone (one meter from the boards). He went in head first! While he lay on the ice, I could see the fear in his eyes. He was crying. I had delivered him a major concussion.

Even at this young age, I didn't like what I had seen and how I could easily hurt someone. It changed the way I played hockey for the rest of my life, forever making me unable to hit people the way my coaches wanted me to. It implanted yet another fear in me that I had to worry about—the fear of hurting others, which was something I was not about. I was a caring person just like my mother.

It was a puzzling dilemma at the time that my brother had no fear, yet I was the opposite and worried about the consequences of every little action. It never made sense to me how someone could just do things and have no regrets. I loved this idea. I had a curse of thinking way too deeply, making my mind micromanage things by risk. I would drive myself insane with the most outrageous things out of this fear I had deep inside.

I would worry about if my parents died, and even counted how many years I thought they had left in their lives. I could never fully live my life because I was always plagued with this constant fear of "what if this, what if that" happened, when I should have just kept moving forward. Some might say I'm a visionary because I worry so much about the future and what our actions will lead to in the future. I witnessed so much destruction through my brother that it was hard to not look at life through this lens.

With things like death always on your mind, it can be depressing. I was never depressed, just a little uneasy. When my friends would want to do something risky, I was always the first person to tell them not to because I measured things by risk and what could happen (don't get me wrong—I did stupid things too). It took me until this time in my life, now in my twenties, that I finally acknowledged it would be better not to focus on death, but on life! You will not know when you're dead anyways, right?

I finally started to open my eyes and believe in myself that "we as people are all equal in that we are given a brain, body, breathe and bleed." We just need people to understand and push a movement that changes the individualist mindset. I am going to lead this movement! We must have a motivational attitude with a perception of change. An attitude that screams, "I am too motivated." The more I drove myself nuts by taking things that people said to me personally, the weaker it made me. The criticism chipped away at me slowly when I should have loved it and let it motivate me to better myself. It was like looking in a mirror at myself and picking out all the flaws I had to fix in my life.

Now, in this time of progression and growth in my life, I have finally begun to open my eyes to see the world for what it is. It's a world run by fear and manipulation. As I said in Chapter 2, the way to beat this is to take a fear and turn it into a positive action. Rather than being scared, I challenge myself. I stopped listening to all of the negatives that people expressed and turned them into positive change. I used it to light a motivational flame inside me to prove people wrong while illustrating that it can be done.

Do not listen to all the statistics that people talk about. Get out there and experience things for yourself. Get a taste of the real world by conversing with as many people as you can to open your eyes and observe what makes them tick. Observe the world in front of you. In doing this, I lost that the fear of myself (like Franklin D. Roosevelt said, "the only thing we have to fear is fear itself"). I finally came to see what needs to be done in this world.

We need to help motivate one another, especially those who live without parents or just have one, as they have it much harder. People who are struggling mentally, physically, emotionally, and financially. In doing this, you're helping people change their mindset! It's not hard to see those struggling. With knowledge and the help of one another, people can overcome adversity by digging themselves out of the hole they are stuck in.

It doesn't take someone to hit rock bottom to figure this out. We can learn from other people's mistakes. We can acquire their knowledge and apply it to a corrective path. Use other people's points of reference as a guide in your life. Still, try to gain as much experience as you can, but just remember some things are common sense. The basic concept of life is that humans only have so much time. This is a positive thing and it forces change for those that want to make a difference in real time. It means we must make the best of what we have and do as much as possible while at the same time helping the less fortunate along the way.

It's time to fill in the gaps that plague the people who are unable to do anything about their predicament. Imagine if we spent all the money used on warfare and negative things to promote a message of peace. What could happen?

That is not to say we will give everything to the people struggling, however we can help the people struggling understand what they are up against and help them build a self-sustaining platform to enable them to move forward. We need everyone to wake up and notice this is possible. Like Will Smith said, *"When we realistically think this is merely not enough, we are going to achieve little. But if we think unrealistically, then the magic is going to happen. The Wright brothers flying metal through the air was unrealistic. A man walking on the moon and going into space was unrealistic. Walking into a room and flicking a light on is unrealistic." - I paraphrased what Will Smith said.* Anyways, back to my story. Since a young age, I was grateful to live with a variety of people from all different parts of the world. From relatives to hockey players to criminals, each would live with my family for a year or so. This gave me a complete different living environment than the usual nuclear household. With this, I wasn't living your average everyday life. The first person to live with us was my Uncle Ernie. This guy never played by the rules and was not a follower of the establishment.

He has passed away now but showed me that you should do what you want to and that there is nothing wrong with this. He did as he felt and didn't listen to the voices of others, which made him such a fun, charismatic person to be around. He wasn't your usual uncle; he was a complete piece of work. Even though I was young when he lived with my family, I caught on that he was good at playing around the rules so that he could get what he wanted. I grasped the message from him that in doing certain things we should not worry about the consequences—although growing up I still did.

A few years later, one of my outgoing aunts moved in for three months—my crazy Aunt Rhonda. Talk about the queen of drama, she is the epitome of this. At the age of twenty-two, she moved to California to pursue a career in modeling and acting. There she was, able to interact and live amongst some of the greatest stars and actors. She lived there for almost nine years, but as it's hard to live in Hollywood. She was unable to secure an acting career. She learned it was a difficult lifestyle and only some are able to make this happen.

Once she moved back, she moved in with my family and set a different dynamic around my house with her charisma. She influenced me to see that, if at the young age of twenty-two she was able to live amongst the stars in Hollywood, I would be able to accomplish and go anywhere in life. She went there too early and I knew that.

Had she waited until she grew up more, maybe the results would have been different. As of now, she is writing a novel—she gave me some inspiration toward how to write and use certain themes of literacy to my advantage. As time passed, she moved on and into her own apartment, leaving my family with a different perspective, especially me. She helped me see what I was capable of doing and encouraged me to pursue my dreams.

Time passed and my dad was building a new hockey club and was unable to secure a place for a hockey player he was bringing in, so we decided he would move in with our family. Garrett Nystedt was a kid from Sault Ste. Marie who was a good hockey player and could put the puck in the net. He actually treated me well, which was a change from every other hockey player I had met thus far, with the exception of a few.

He was entering high school as I was entering grade seven middle school, so we both had different ideas about what was going on. He was able to enter high school and make new friends quiet easily, which showed me as long as you are a nice person, how could anyone hate you? Obviously, we can see a different reality in this world, but watching him allowed me time to grow and feel more comfortable talking to people older than myself.

Things didn't work out for Garrett as he became homesick and ended up leaving within a few months. The one nice thing about the kid was that he was never angry—it didn't seem as if he had an angry bone in his body, which was a change and great to see.

After he left, it was time for my family to live a normal dynamic so we decided to take a break from billeting. We were already busy enough with hockey because my dad was always the manager of my brother's hockey teams and my mom did all the convening for the leagues. From a young age, it was always go, go, and go. We had a unique family dynamic where we wouldn't always sit at the dinner table. We would rather watch television or do our own thing. It was a special aspect of my life because we were not like the usual family; we were all different and we all felt very close to one another.

For so long I had wished we were like normal families doing other things, until years down the line I had come to understand what we had. I always wanted things I didn't have that other families did, when I should have just been grateful for what I was given—a unique bond consisting of safety and love.

All families are different and this is what makes that aspect of someone's life so special. My family never ran on any schedule; we just did things as they needed to get done. It wasn't as if we were unorganized, we were just happy with how we were living so there was no need for a schedule.

We all had our own special attributes that made us do things differently. My father, who was the leader of the house, kept everything structured and provided the safety. My mom was the lover who cared about everything and never judged anyone for anything. She was always there when we needed support or an ear to talk to. Then there was my brother who was the elite athlete. People may not have thought he was the best hockey player but that was because they were envious of the skills he possessed, including that mental edge he had over any of them. He may not have been the best puck handler, but he sure as hell made up for it in every other aspect of the game. Lastly there was me—the different one.

I was always the visionary, never stopping the belief that one day I would take everything over and support the family as I aspire to do (and will not stop until is all said and done). I am the motivator of the family, the one who only wants to enable everyone to be the best they can be, including myself. As it turned out, the family dynamic changed once again as my brother came back home from playing hockey in Chicoutimi (he was always moving around with hockey). My father was involved in this new Junior A hockey league and needed to bring in international hockey players to Canada.

When this happened, we were supposed to have a billet from Germany named Christoph Heinz move in with us. On the day Christoph moved in, another player from California showed up in our driveway—a player my brother had played with from California had dropped him off so we had no choice but to take him in. I still remember me and my mom looking out the window and saying, "Why is this kid unpacking from Jake's (brother's friend) car?"

His name was Blaise Decfic, a Hungarian from Los Angeles, California. We now had a German and a Californian living at our house as well as my mom, dad, brother, and myself. What a different environment to live in, as we are all from different parts of the globe. Once we became familiar with each other, it was a great experience. We called Blaise "Blazer" because when he drove our vehicle he would drive all over the place—I guess he was used to those California freeways.

Christoph was more of a soft-hearted person who was deeply in love with his girlfriend. It always cracked me up because she definitely had him whipped even though he lived so far away. He had moved from British Columbia but he was originally from Germany. There was no such thing as being bored in my household. It was like a zoo—there was always excitement around the house.

Literately there were always people in my house. After hockey games, a bunch of them would pile into my house and metaphorically wreck the place. It wasn't always the best because my mom would do groceries and everything would be destroyed within a day, due to the fact that they were big, growing hockey players.

With these guys, I had the opportunity to meet people from England, Arizona, and all different parts of Canada and the globe. The nice thing about these billets was that they allowed me to hang out with them. They would take me to the gym with them to work out and show me the tricks of the trade on becoming a smart hockey player.

Living with these people helped me advance my social skills as I was always communicating with people older than me, learning to understand life from all angles. In a way, you could say it made me see things differently than kids my age. It was nice for once that people accepted me.

One time when my parents were out of town for hockey they had a car they were holding at our house, an old Cadillac Deville. I found the keys for the car and for some reason I thought it would be a great idea to take it for a spin and pick up some of my friends.

With no prior driving experience, I went and picked up my buddy who lived up the street. We had a problem though—I needed gas and had no license if I got caught. Anyways, my friend and I decided to go fill up a tank—well fifteen bucks worth because I was only fourteen at the time. My friend hopped out because he wanted to try to get cigarettes while I filled up.

Little did we know it was an old-school car and if you leave the keys in the cup holder with the windows up, the car would lock. Here I am, fourteen years old, trying to unlock this car and the girl at the cash is asking me if I have CAA to be able to come unlock it. I'm thinking to myself, I don't even have a license how could I have CAA?

I decided to go to the Mr. Lube across the street to ask for assistance. Luckily, I met a guy who said he had broken into cars without door handles, so I felt in good hands. Within twenty seconds this guy unlocked the door and I was forever grateful. I gave him five dollars because that's all I had left from the fifteen I spent on gas. What a crazy experience that was and when my parents came back they never suspected a thing.

Still to this day, I don't know why I was stupid enough to do this. Live and learn, I guess. I still remember when I first pulled onto the main road that day and was thinking "oh boy."

There were plenty of times like this living with these billets. Since they were always out of town with my parents, I was able to have the house to myself and do certain things I wanted to. Once the year was over the billets were heading home and it was a sad time because we as a family grew attached to living with these people. They were like brothers to us. Christoph and Blaze gave me different tools I could use in my life when dealing with people. This experience allowed me to relax when talking and have a normal conversation (even though I did not). It was a nice phase of my life because I always had someone to talk to who wasn't part of the family who could give me feedback about life.

I had also lived with a guy named Dan Garneau. He is like a second brother to me. He's travelled with my family and spent Christmas with us when he had nowhere to go. This guy may not have played hockey but he sure knew it better than most people. He was a scout who would bring players in to this new Junior A hockey league. He was from Alberta and was such a caring guy. He was great to talk to and even, ironically, set me up with a few ladies. Anyways, Danny got a new job and moved on with his life. I see him from time to time.

Finally, with all these people I had lived with, from this point on I started cracking out of my shell. Now my family went back to normal, just the four of us again. It was nice to finally have peace and quiet because my house was always so alive. At times it was okay, but it would get quite annoying because there was always this feeling that someone was at the house. I always had school in the morning and these guys would be up until three or four in the morning.

The terrible thing with all the hockey was the fact that all the hockey parents were consumed by smoking cigarettes. It was sad in a way that after ever period everyone would go out for a "dart" break. I think this kept me away from smoking—I couldn't stand it. It was just gross how an addiction could take over people as it did with these parents. To this day, I'm grateful I don't smoke—it's a waste of time, like sucking back an exhaust pipe. I lived with another person from Newfoundland we called Mack. He was another one addicted to nicotine. The guy would go through 75% of a tin of tobacco at a time.

I also lived with another kid from Alberta named Jared. He was a great guy and hockey player too. He showed me lots of cool tricks because we played the same position in hockey. The funniest thing I remember about him was that he would swallow the tobacco after chewing it—it was the most bizarre thing. He was an outgoing ladies' man who had a great personality.

The funny thing was, I ended up signing to the same Junior A hockey team Jared was on until I found out the first game we were playing was against my brother's team. I then quit the team because I knew my brother would kill me. He even called me and reminded me he was going to clean the ice with me. What a great brother, eh?

Something that I grasped from Jared was his encouragement and positive attitude. Nothing could really bring this kid down. I applied it successfully to my life once he moved out.

The last person who moved in with my family was one of my brother's friends who had been kicked out of his house. He was a tough-looking guy but was honestly a great person. I was lucky enough to have come across him and for him to share his street smarts with me. This was the type of guy you don't mess with—he had a big rep backing him up. The sad reality was that he was a recovering drug addict going through his own struggles in life so that he could become clean.

Out of any of my brother's friends, he was the easiest to talk to and I could see that deep down inside all he wanted to do was make a change in his life. The only problem was that he was playing a tough game and it takes time to recover, as he was on methadone treatments. For someone who looked like a gangster, with his diamond stud earrings and tattoos, it was not the attitude he portrayed. It was evident he was a loving, caring human being. He lived with my family for little over a year, and even after my brother moved away for hockey.

Finally, the time came for him to face his fear and go home to his dad.

The sad reality was that he suddenly died about two years later in his sleep from unknown causes. He was like a brother to not only me but also to my brother Ryan. It was one of the hardest losses we had to go through as a family because we knew how much of a caring person he was. It was sad because I only remember a bleak memory of seeing him eight months before his death and it was a hello, good-bye sort of deal.

I really bonded with him because he was into the martial arts scene, as was I. I will never forget him. I am truly blessed with the knowledge and street smarts he gave me throughout my life. I know he would laugh about this now but he showed me courage through his struggles. What I took from him was never to put myself into or involve myself in the things he had done, to learn from his mistakes to not only better myself but to become wiser. To be smart, react, and don't get myself killed, and to keep my mouth shut (although I have a hard time with the last one).

Another big chapter of my life revolves around sports—they have helped me become the person I am today. Contact sports have been a big part of my life because they were ideal for me. I hated soccer as it was too soft and I didn't like that we were unable to use our hands. I was born and raised a hockey player with ten years in the sport. I loved it but it wasn't my passion as I grew up, so I quit at the age of sixteen. I played tennis, which looks much easier than it is to direct the ball to go where you want it to, but it was good for learning mental and physical coordination.

I played lacrosse for three years, playing rep for one year, which is more advanced. I would have gone on with this sport, but I lacked the motivation at the time. I should have just progressed instead of being so lazy. I hope you begin to see why laziness is a weakness and a killer. Just go for something or at least attempt it. This will give you much more fulfillment in life. To this day I still remember scoring a goal one game while pulling my pants up with one hand and curling my stick with the other. It was phenomenal—I somehow dodged and hit through five different players to get the goal. My mom was keeping score at the time and the ref said to her, "Number seven scored pulling up his pants."

I also enjoyed the game of golf, which I still play when I am able to because it's difficult and relaxing at the same time. I find chipping is the hardest part of the game as I can drive an easy two hundred and twenty yards on a good day. I still remember this one time on vacation with my dad when I drove the ball at least two hundred and twenty yards (with these expensive rental clubs) in Myrtle Beach, South Carolina. It hit the siding of someone's house on the course, knocking a piece of it off.

Anyways, I have always had lots of fun on the golf course. A long time ago my good friend and I thought it would be a good idea to take the golf carts out in the winter when this golf course down his street was closed (actually, he didn't think it was the greatest idea but I assured him everything would be alright).

There we were, driving on this golf course with two pellet guns going hunting for geese. Then all of a sudden, we saw the owner of the course with two of his kids. Boy, what a shock that was, so my buddy waved at the owner, all normal, and we kept on driving. I still remember to this day his dog running over the hill and thinking, "This can't be good." The owner lost it on us and banned us from the golf course.

Luckily, he didn't get the police involved. Years later I called and apologized, which he accepted and allowed us both back on the course. This was complete stupidity but a funny story to show why not to do stupid things and how decisions have consequences. Anyways, I later tried out football in high school, which I wasn't too fond of. It was enjoyable with all my friends but I was running the ball one time and someone put their helmet full tilt right into my bicep making me unable to feel my arm for a couple seconds. After that, I wasn't too enthusiastic about the sport.

I couldn't get around the concept that we run from one end of the field full tilt and clash into each other, mimicking some aspect of war. After playing football for two years and getting over hockey, I switched gears. Entering into grade eleven in high school, I decided to try out the sport of Muay Thai. I was playing the UFC 09 video game and really wanted to try out MMA. I had always been interested in it, as I had tried karate as a young kid. My parents thought it was a waste of time and money because it was across the city. After finally convincing them, it turned out to be my passion (rather than doing boxing, my bro had said to look up Muay Thai).

When I first started, I was there four times a week because I was so eager to gain knowledge. If I didn't go, I would lose it and become upset. Muay Thai is the art of the eight limbs, a sport based out of Thailand that the Thai warriors used to use on the battlefield. In my opinion, it's the most complete stand-up martial art because it uses everything from elbows, knees, kicks, punches, and the clinch. It delivers the best cardio and most mentally grueling workout of any combat sport, in my opinion.

I've tried most of the combat sports and this is the one that I love. I used to annoy everyone with the passion I had for the sport, as it was all I would talk about. I recommend it to anyone who thinks they can fight and likes to fight on the street because street fighting is a waste of time— prize fighting's the real deal. At least coming to train and fight in a ring it's a sanctioned environment where you learn respect and discipline, rather than hurting someone else for the fun of it. It's also great for self-defense. The funny thing is, I was never a fighter, my brother always was.

From a young age, I was always interested in the art of fighting, watching Dragonball Z, Teenage Mutant Ninja Turtles, and the Karate Kid. The other odd thing is I didn't like getting hurt in football, yet in Muay Thai you're dealing with kicks to the head and knees to the solar plexus, which doesn't bother me at all.

It was one of the best choices I could have ever made because in my opinion, it gave me a sixth sense. Why I say this is because your body and brain are your weapons and tools of attack. Most of the time, it's the smarter fighter who beats a stronger opponent because they are stronger mentally. An example of this is pro wrestling legend Dan Gable. He is known for loving to fight people who abused steroids because he knew he could mentally break them down.

Obviously, anyone can get caught because we are all human, but if you fight smart it can give you an edge against an angry opponent swinging for the fences. The art also teaches you about your own body and brain, educating you to use them while fighting to make quick decisions (being able to react).

Fighting has been part of human nature since the dawn of time. It literally gave me motivation more than anything else ever had. It awakened the sleeping giant. If kids would only recognize that they can set a goal and go compete in the ring, rather than going around hurting others in the streets, gaining nothing from it and potentially getting charged or go to jail. I am going to be involved in the art for the rest of my life because it has kept me fit and in my opinion gave me a mental edge over other types of athletes. It makes you push past those limits that people think are unbreakable and helps greatly with endurance as well.

Pain becomes irrelevant and it can help alleviate fear in your life enabling you to gain confidence. The funny thing about fighting to for anyone against it is the fact that when someone sees a fight they will watch it. Someone could be having sex in the street, but if there is a fight happening in front of them, they will more than likely watch the fight. I was lucky enough to compete in eight demonstrations, unsanctioned fights and one national title fight to test my abilities and I will say they were unbelievable. I should have more fights but fear has a funny way of interfering with things.

I did get hurt against a 27-year-old, who I rocked and he got angry so he rocked me back. I was all right, it just was unsanctioned, not amateur fighting, so they stopped the fight when I was bleeding all over the ring. Boy, was that interesting. My dad, who deals with insurance, wasn't too happy about it and would have shut it all down if it were not for me.

I still remember the one doctor looking at me and saying I was all right and my dad snapping, calling him an idiot because my pupils were dilated and I was dazed (huge liability). Fighting gives you a natural adrenaline and a heightened awareness making you feel alive. I was also able to compete in the national championships and received a silver metal. I could have won a title belt but was too lazy. The fact was, I didn't train nearly enough and paid the price by getting caught with my hand down too low in the first fifteen seconds.

Think about this: your fight just starts, then—bang—you're rocked and all you're thinking about is survival and trying not to get knocked out. Fear plagued me the rest of the fight because I had to recover from my brain being like scrambled eggs. I learned my lesson and realized that if you are fully prepared you will have less stress and be able to perform with less worry. Although I finished all three rounds, I still to this day don't remember walking back to the dressing room. I should have at least ten more fights on my record but sticking to a decision and not backing out of fights has been a weakness of mine. This only happens when it comes to fighting because I am a very peaceful person. I know for a fact what I can do to people in there so I have no reason to prove it by kicking someone in the head and making them go to sleep, or the same happening to me.

I always remember the television commercial in which the Frosted Flakes tiger said practice makes perfect. By doing this, all your tools will be sharper rather than being unprepared as I had been. It's the same in life; if you don't prepare for something like a speech and "wing it" you will more than likely not succeed as you would had you rehearsed it over and over. The same goes for a lawyer; a person could know the law in and out, but another lawyer could have a better case prepared and take over.

There's nothing wrong with being over-prepared for something because then you will be ready for anything that is thrown at you. When you are not prepared, you can get caught in a spot not knowing how to properly calculate your next move and someone can catch on to this. Like my opponent catching me off guard in my national fight.

I've found that the more prepared I am for something, the less fear I will have and this will reflect better results. Think about this: all we as humans do is produce results, whether negative or positive. Failure or success. Back in school, everyone used to laugh at this kid in my class who tried so hard but produced results. I bet now he's having the last laugh with his study habits and work ethic. Learning from other professionals is also great because they are people who have dogged it out and produced results. This is why my martial arts technique has developed so far.

I've had great trainers and training partners. People like Kru Chris Kew who has trained many champions and is a world champion himself. Ajahn Berklertk, who is like the Muhammad Ali of Muay Thai, with 70 or more fights in Thailand. He didn't even speak English but his technique was so strong that you could gain something from him.

Kru Jeff, a professional MMA fighter, Mark "Boots" Holst, another professional MMA and Thai boxer, Jean Charles Skarbowsky, who is a French Thai boxer with unbelievable technique in the art and had an attitude of "just do it" rather than ask questions, and Nate Diaz, who was the former number one contender in the UFC lightweight division—each have all have taught me so much.

Even my first two trainers were unbelievable and pushed me to my limits—their names are Mike Houle and Jessie Cronier. Had I not gone to the same gym they were training at, I wouldn't have as much knowledge of the art as I do now, or maybe I would have never thought of fighting. The great thing about them being my first trainers in the art was the fact that they were both around my age, so it was easy to learn off them. I now would easily be able to run a hard cardio workout with all the skills I acquired from them.

The old gym I first participated at started having issues and kicking members out so I parted ways and moved on. It wasn't ideal because a solid team had been shattered. I would have dreams about us all reuniting with one another to train again.

Oddly enough, one day came when a gym called Team Shredder welcomed us aboard their squad. This team was a hard-core gym, running under the guidance of Yve Charette, who had 25-plus years of martial arts experience. He is the Greg Jackson (famous MMA coach) of Northern Ontario. This gym is by far the most complete MMA gym in Sudbury Ontario, with a BJJ black belt—they don't build winners, they build champions.

Had I not started training with Yve, I wouldn't be nearly as mentally strong as I am today. The guy is a complete machine who brings charisma to each class he directs. He bred the only UFC fighter in Sudbury named Mitch Gagnon, who I have been lucky enough to train with. This just goes to show the caliber of athletes Yve builds in his gym.

You can feel a presence walking into his gym—that there are no excuses; what you're going to get out of your workout is all about what you put in. Hard work is key. Train hard and honest. With this, martial arts has opened up a variety of different doors in my life because it promotes the right morals.

Yve has showed me this and in my opinion, he is the best at delivering mentally grueling workouts that make a person learn not to quit, rather to laugh when something gets hard and want more of it. The only reason I have not fought under Yve is, like I said, I let fear of my past stop me from doing so. As of now, it's all I have been working on, as he told me to attack this fear head-on and step-by-step—it's what I'm doing to achieve this goal.

One thing I can say about martial arts is that it's allowed me to train with a variety of professional athletes much easier than in any other sport. MMA fighters, in a sense, are easier to train with in the type of sport environment they are involved in. I'm not saying this is always the case, but I played hockey for over ten years and only got to train with two professionals: Bryan Trottier, who was the assistant captain of the New York Islanders (and won 7 Stanley Cups to boot), as well as Jim Dorey (who I consider an uncle), who held the record for most penalty minutes in the NHL for a long time.

I believe MMA fighters do not get enough credit, as they destroy their bodies and put it all on the line when they fight. Fighters take each other's heads off and can get severely hurt, yet don't make as much as boxers do.

All these people I have been able to meet have driven my inspiration to exponential levels because it goes to show if they were able to persevere, then why can't I if work hard enough at something? I believe life's true values are discipline, patience, hard work, passion and, when a person becomes sick of going through the motions, perseverance. Perfect Napoleon Hill's burning desire with an obsessive mentality toward what you are doing. Just drive every day; do as much as you can. I have issues with patience. It irritates me but I am learning how to control this irritation. Breathing and visualizing the future and how my strategy will unfold. Notice how I said "will" and not "if".

This has to happen in order to perfect something rather than moving on to something else. Another great thing I learned from my trainer Yve Charette is the fact that he never does the same workouts twice. It will always be something different so that no muscle memory is built and the body will not become bored repeating the same workouts over and over again. If there is no pain, there is no gain. This way the body is always reacting to something different, rather than the same old routines.

At times, you begin to question your trainer's style until you throw something like a kick and realized it is beneficial, or go for a run with no thought of every quitting.

The lessons learned in class carry through into the real world as well. All of the senses become awakened when training at Team Shredder. All these ideas go to show you that if you put in the work it will benefit you in the end. Yes, you may be uncomfortable at the time, but it's better than sitting on the couch day dreaming about it. Trust me, I've done too much of this, so now it's my biggest goal to train at least four times a week. Now I incorporate weight lifting to add power to my training routine. I used to hate it but now I have the right mindset towards it. Results take time. It's an accumulation process. You may not see results in a month or three but wait a year down the line and your eyes will become opened. You may think thirty minutes a day of reading is nothing, well add that up over seven days a week. Imagine in a year from now how many hours you will have booked.

It helps relieve that fear that we all have of dreading a workout when you just have to get it over with. We as humans never got anywhere sitting around waiting for something to happen—we went out there and got what we wanted. Turning the negative of doing nothing into a positive of doing something. Giving up and quitting never moved any aspect of life forward.

Sure, it gave people ways to cheat and find shortcuts to get something done faster, but the reality is that it's that hard work ethic that will benefit us as humans. It's better to keep failing than not to try at all. Failing is just experience. The ability to work hard is a great thing to have when everyone else is sitting on the sidelines making observations.

It's time for people to get the notification and start innovating. Create change in the things we are able to control. As I mentioned, we can control our attitude. Look at Mitch Gagnon, a UFC fighter from a small mining town in Ontario. Doubters probably thought he wouldn't make it, but now he's the only UFC fighter from Sudbury. His hard work, day in and day out, the grueling physical and mental workouts, paid off in the end because his dreams came true.

The same premise can be effectively applied to your life. When you keep getting knocked down, get back up because if you don't, then fear has done its job to defeat you. It has made you quit and sucked the life right out of you rather than motivating you to get back up and stand tall, to encourage you to gain something from your losses. We move forward because we make mistakes and learn from them so that we do not repeat ourselves.

If you give up and quit on yourself, you will either regret it or try harder next time. I don't believe in the saying, 'once a quitter, always a quitter'. I believe rather in the fact that either you stay a quitter, or you become a winner.

Might I remind you that you should be ecstatic you are alive right now? Some people are fighting in wars and loosing limbs while others are struggling to support their families and live day by day. No one controls your mind, only you. This is where a big change in my life happened and nothing would have made sense without the insights I just gave you. There are a significant number of things I left out, but this is a motivational book, not a book about dark things—it's about overcoming obstacles.

I used to make thousands of excuses about why I was unable to do something until I realized the easiest solution is just doing something. It's better to go to a workout and get it over with even if you are not pushing yourself than to not go at all. We waste the same amount of energy thinking up excuses rather than just making an attempt. I will emphasis this at the end of the book but some people's excuses are embarrassing when there are people in wheelchairs struggling every day to live a normal life. This is where reality finally hit and I understood life would never be the same. It opened my eyes to the real world that is in front of us, our vulnerable planet. The power of change was bestowed upon me.

At times, life can seem too perfect, as if things are going to stay the same forever. As kids, we breathe this reality and when the shit hits the fan, it becomes hard to adapt to a new reality. We as humans have a hard time dealing with change because it's something we are unaccustomed to. We like keeping things the way they are because it makes us happy, instead of getting out in the world and discovering what it has to offer. The problem is, the majority of people don't like leaving the comfort zone. In order to avoid meritocracy in life, the comfort zone must be put aside.

For most of my life I had felt this way; I was oblivious to the reality of the world in front of me. I would worry about other people but not about the true power of life and change. Then entering into grade twelve my parents decided to divorce. It was something I never thought would happen. I was so blind to the fact that they could ever split up. I had always seen my parents as perfect together because they were always helping other people's relationships. It was something that never even crossed my mind until I got slapped in the face with reality.

I will never forget the day my mom went away for a weekend and finally got the strength to leave my father. As a married couple, both my parents had been through enough and my mom worked up the strength to leave. People don't understand how hard it was for my mom to leave, but I do and it sure takes a lot of courage to leave something built so strong.

One day my dad came to my work and asked me if I was able to go home. I thought at the time my great-grandmother was dying, as she had been in the hospital. My manager let me go home and I met my dad where he sat me down. I had no idea what to expect. He said to me, "Connor, I don't know how to tell you this, but your mother has left me and I don't know what to do." This was the first time I ever heard my father say he did not know what to do.

He was sued by one of the biggest Insurance companies in the United States and won his case, and now he was telling me he doesn't know what to do. The man who kept all the drama in my family together and the years of hard work he put in to get me where I am today, didn't know where to turn. It was powerful yet like a slap in the face as I heard it and my whole jaw went completely numb in disbelief.

It was a feeling that was incomprehensible because, like I said, I did not see a thing coming. Let us not forget that my mother had a big piece in all of this, as she was the one with all the love that will never be forgotten. Money can't buy a smile like hers.

We really had something special like every family does, so when you have something this wonderful all those years, all those trips together as a family unit, it's hard to face reality. I watched my dad break down, something I had thought was impossible. I couldn't believe what had just happened and it even took me two years to realize my mother was not coming home. I still see her all the time but just the fact that they were not together anymore was hard to believe.

My brain for so many years was used to them being together, so close it's embarrassing. Still to this day, I dream of them together. It has been more than four years, but still, there was nothing like the day it actually happened. My mother, one of the most peaceful women to walk this planet, did something unexpected. It was just madness. I cannot blame her for this, as it was a two-way street and change is inevitable. In reality, I got to see my parents for who they really were, which was a change.

In the end, I can understand now that my father lives a stressful life that some people are unable to handle, so she was at her wits' end. I still remember going to school the next day and someone saying to me I wouldn't be able to hand my assignment in late and I almost lost it. I said to that person, "Well yeah, my parents just split. You don't think this is a good enough excuse?"

I had always been a very happy, charismatic, positive person and now I'd had to deal with this. I wasn't sure which route to go because I hadn't dealt with anything of this caliber before. I decided to go with the "I don't care" attitude and just accept the fact that this is the ways it was going to be—just brush it off and roll with it because in the past things worked out. I kept that smile shining bright and treated my mom terribly. I didn't step in her shoes to see that she was unhappy at the time.

I couldn't comprehend what was happening to my family or even wrap my head around it to understand why. The problem with the attitude I chose to go with was that I had too many mixed emotions. I was unable to face reality. This just made things worse in the end because it was harder to accept the situation I was in. It made me stuck on the question of how I had something for so long and then it was all gone.

I finally came to terms with the reality of the change I was involved in. I snapped back into focus and was wide awake to what was in front of me. I came to the realization that everything that had happened was a positive not a negative. Stuff like this needs to happen for people to fully appreciate what they have and to not take things for granted. You can never go back into a moment once previously lived. I couldn't keep asking myself, if I had known my mom wanted to leave, would I have been able to convince her otherwise?

I was never really close to my father before as he was always so busy with my brother. I was a mama's boy and always will be. My mother is the sweetest, warm-hearted woman and that was why I didn't see her leaving. She was always good at hiding things. For example, when her mother got diagnosed with cancer three days before Christmas she kept it from me and my brother until after Christmas was over, allowing us to enjoy our Christmas.

Back to the positive though. Now I'm closer to my father than ever and still just as close with my mother. The only problem was, when my mom left she thought I'd be moving in with her but I just couldn't do that to my dad when he was at his lowest hour (as was she). I wanted to stay in the house we built our lives together in. My dad offered me the choice to stay with my mom in the house. I declined because it just wasn't right. I didn't know at the time my mother needed support, not just my father. I didn't comprehend that what she did was exceptionally hard to do.

Positive results followed all that anger and I never forgot the love and care she showed me, which is why I could never abandon her. All four members of my family's names are outside my house in the concrete and now there are only two of us left. All in all, I don't see negative energy in this because I don't know where I would be now had they stayed together.

We are all in good places now with a positive energy. My dad has a great girlfriend and my mom has a great boyfriend. I don't care who they are with as long as they are happy—that is all that matters to me. As much as I would love to have it all go back to normal, this is not a possibility; we are all set in our ways for the better. No regrets. Life is pushing forward with no drama. Over time, the scars have healed and the wounds have faded.

Some people will always have a label put on my brother for some of the things he has done in his life. The fact is, he learned from his mistakes and is one of the most positive influences in my life. Without my brother, I wouldn't be who I am today. I wouldn't be the love-filled caring person I was molded into without that guy. He made me mentally stronger and allowed me to understand the world at a more accelerated pace. He has done things that other people cannot even comprehend and taught me a valuable lesson about life: that you can sink to the deepest of lows and dig yourself from underneath that dirt. He has a beautiful girlfriend and daughter now. Sometimes people try to bring negativity into his life, but that doesn't matter to him.

He doesn't live in the past. He is now where he needs to be. He went from a heart full of hate to a caring individual who doesn't want to hurt anyone. He is a true inspiration. He taught me that you can be someone and then flip the card and turn out to be someone great. I thank him for everything he has done for me. It may sound like he is a bad guy in the beginning of all this but we have always been very close. Closer than any of my friends, we share a special bond that no one will understand unless they have a brother. The only difference is he is my brother and no one can take that away from me. He just needs to stop feeling sorry for the things he has done and use it as his motivation. But that's life's lesson, which I have emphasized—choices are everything.

Anyone who can try to bring a negative to the positive things that happened to my family is just showing their own weakness, because every family has their struggles. My family was close enough to keep the bond we had together strong. Anyone who knocks my mom down for what she did doesn't know what they are even talking about because they weren't walking in her shoes, living the life she had; they were living their own lives. This is why premature judgment is meaningless because it does nothing but proves pure negligence. In my life this was a big issue, but in reality it was nothing compared to some of the things people get put through. This opened my mind up to the real potential I possess and that some people are living in much worse situations than my own. I must be grateful and work hard to make a difference, to help those in need.

After high school I did not end up getting into university because my average was too low. I ended up taking the year off and did some travelling with my father, allowing me some down time and the opportunity to contemplate life. What I came to realize with all that time off was that I did not want to be working a minimum wage job and that all my desires could be accomplished as long as I kept a positive mental attitude working towards my goals.

 I was told by the high school guidance teacher I would need two marks over eighty-five percent to be able to get into university. It turns out, I got in with only taking one class scoring an eighty-five. I was so determined to get into university that I knew nothing was going to stop me. I finally understood what I wanted to do with my life. In taking that year off school, I thought I was wasting time, although if I had went I probably would have been wasting money. The good thing with all of this is I got to understand myself and the basic fundamentals of life, how each of us possesses skills to be able to help one another and grow to the highest level, like a tree in the forest. I now appreciate school more than ever and enjoy every day I get to partake in courses and enhance my knowledge. Remember, each of us have the basic fundamentals to produce change within our lives. The power of making a decision is something no money can buy. Set yourself a standard that can act as a guideline towards what you will accept and what you will not accept.

 I believe that, to an extent, things happen for a reason. We as humans have a choice to choose how we write our story and the choices we make will reflect our conscious decisions. Certain things are out of our control, but inevitably "something" is going to happen as a reflection of the past positive or negative—a reflection of the choices we make. You chose to get up in the morning or lay in bed. You must encode the things you desire within your subconscious mind and become obsessive over them. Think and act the way you want people to perceive you and it will become you.

 I could play twenty questions wondering what would have happened if my parents didn't split and the answer is, I like where it ended up. I feel the one reason it worked out was because of the fact that we as a family held the belief that it would all work out in the end. If my parents had stayed together it possibly wouldn't have been real, just something fictional. Now my parents get along better than when they were together. Ironically enough, they own the same insurance company together. Say the things you want to hear! Start acting and showcasing yourself to the world by being the person you want to become!

The experience I gained from this was that I had to grow up a little faster and face what was in front of me. I couldn't run away and hide this time, which was new for me. My life is now right where I want it to be. It always had been but now I was wide awake to the world in front of me. I see goals in front of me and the things that I need to work toward, rather than wasting my time doing nothing. I now appreciate things for what they are and do not take anything for granted. I never set a goal in my life until I was nineteen, and was I ever missing out.

I am thankful for every minute I get to spend with my parents now, instead of sitting in the basement doing nothing. It took that hardship to finally make me realize the true beauty in this world. The fact is, things are going to happen in each and every one of our lives and if we curl up and die then we fail at life. If, instead, we take them as experience and bumps in the road we will be able to grow and better ourselves as people. There is no point dwelling on something that could have been when we are capable of creating new beginnings that are even better than the ones that stood before us.

Enjoy every day that you create your story. Be who you are and never look back. Make people notice you and your message. Always remember, nothing lasts forever, so it's your job to react and make the best conscious decisions you can to create the future you want to live in. The only limitations are the ones set within our own conscious realm of thought.

You the reader have the ability to change the world—whoever tells you differently doesn't believe in their full capabilities. By this point in time, "impossible" should not even be a word in your vocabulary. You will start first by influencing individuals, then the world. Do not be scared; it's your turn to take on the world. The key to happiness is to always have something to look forward to, day in and day out. When opportunity arises, don't have a second thought, embrace it and use the power that burns within you. Once you make that decision, nothing is going to stop you.

Don't be afraid to leave your mark on Mother Earth. She will try to break you down and beat you up, but it's your job to get back up and prove to yourself nothing is impossible. Prove to people you can do it, for them to see the truth. Use this as your motivation.

What motivates you?

Connor LaRocque: Writer of this book, Law Student.

My hunger to change the mindset of this world and become a revolutionary innovator of thought. I want to influence people to be fearless in their lives chasing their dreams rather than being told what to do. I want people to perceive things that where some see darkness they can see light. I am starting an equality movement that promotes humanitarian rights and helps make people understand their true potential is burning within each of them.

George Cooke: Former President and CEO Dominion General Insurance Company of Canada and Current Chairman of the Board at OMERS.

I am motivated by people, issues or causes, community, and an attachment to doing the right thing. Public policy has always interested me. It surrounds all that we do and thus is essential to understand and get right.

Like you, I grew up in a Northern community, (mine was smaller than yours) and we all needed to help each other and ourselves to survive. It led to a belief in yourself and what you could do, and how you could give something back to your community or to those who needed help. Interestingly, in my corporate work our culture embraced the notion of doing the right thing and making a difference. We incorporated these notions into our daily routine.

Jim Dorey: Former Toronto Maple Leafs hockey player.

What makes me get up and go in the morning is that I want to I want to do things. I want to accomplish some things, I want to finish something... I want to change some things....Connor, my makeup is a pusher, go getter, I do not every want to not have a reason to get up and move on. It's an eternal drive I have. That's as simple as I get.

Cindy Turcotte: Vice President of Operations at Local Insurance.

Setting a goal that betters ones current situation, whether financially, educationally or personally and then achieving that goal.

Wess Dowsett: Area Coordinator for the Steel Workers Union. Role: Contract negotiating and Dispute resolution.

At the end of the day, we all live setting goals. I don't set myself unrealistic goals. I set for myself achievable goals and what motivates me is achieving realistic goals on a regular basis to keep momentum going. Opportunities are often missed because they are dressed in overalls and look like work

David Kilgour: Teacher.

What motivates me? The desire to wake up every day with the intention to somehow make a difference in at least one way. That could be as simple as helping my community in a fundraising effort or making a change at work that improves the way we do things. Some days, when life is getting a little challenging, it's at least comforting to me that I can make a difference every day, even if it is a small one. For instance, today after a long day at work, I attended the Annual General Meeting of the Sudbury Multicultural and Folk Arts Association. I was there to talk about a project the Star was planning and I connected with five new people I had never met before. We talked about how to improve communication among the different cultures in Sudbury and agreed we should all find new ways of increasing understanding among all cultures in our community. I had no idea this was going to happen when I got up this morning, I only knew I was attending the meeting and that I would try to make a difference in some way. Not sure if I am explaining myself very well, but I suppose my point is that I need to take on the right attitude, a positive attitude every day when I wake up. As I say, sometimes that can be very difficult to do and honestly, it doesn't work for me every day because shit happens but at least I can try every day.

In terms of attitude, I live by the words of an American author and educator Charles Swindoll. I have posted this on my door many times and I always have people asking me for a copy, which I think is great because attitude is a contagious thing. This is what he wrote;

"The longer I live, the more I realize the impact of attitude on life. Attitude, to me, is more important than facts. It is more important than the past, than education, than money, than circumstances, than failures, than successes, than what other people think, say or do. It is more important than appearance, giftedness or skill. It will make or break a company... a church... a home. The remarkable thing is we have a choice every day regarding the attitude we embrace for that day. We cannot change our past... we cannot change the fact that people will act in a certain way. We cannot change the inevitable. The only thing we can do is play the one string we have, and that is our attitude... I am convinced that life is 10% what happens to me and 90% how I react to it.

And so it is with you... we are in charge of our attitudes."

Al Vardy: Financial Advisor

Essentially, I feel motivated when "the future I am living into is one that I very much desire." That is not always the case and when it is not, the intention is to "create possibilities" to help bring that desired future back into the "almost-certain, foreseeable" future. Life is least motivating when it appears that much of what is preventing this from occurring is not perceived or ultimately not within your control, at least not without some significant action such as leaving your employer/spouse after trying all within reason, within your control to alter.

Dr. Christopher Nizzero: Physician/Family Doctor:

Passion keeps me going, I have a big practice so I need to keep learning to provide my patients with the most up to date and relevant information possible to provide the best service.

Dana. M. Cudney: Essential Faculty Dept. of Sociology.

I am motivated by challenges, specifically problem solving. Applied social research provides numerous opportunities to exercise skills in this area.

Yves Charette: Owner of Team Shredder MMA, Osteopathic practitioner and College professor.

What motivates me every day is knowing that I get an opportunity to influence, or motivate someone's life through teaching at the college, helping someone through my osteopathic practice or through martial arts.

Life is Motivation Poetry
By Connor LaRocque

Read my book, *Life is Motivation*, stop sitting on the sidelines making observations, get the notification it's time to start innovating. Not ten years down the line when you finally have your pity realization. By then I'm already going to be elevating because I have education. Rising to higher peaks than Everest with my dedication. Through cooperation, avocations and using the right words in a conversation.

All my life I have wanted to be a true inspiration like JFK, Mahatma Gandhi, Abraham Lincoln and anyone else who was a complete domination. In the eyes of the people there's no time for hesitation, just determination as if we were building a new civilization except it's going to be called my nation, dial up the president, where the fuck's my nomination? I'm starting a new generation with a new type of nationalization, no more limitations only accommodations helping the poor and starving without justification.

Time to tip some bottles in celebration. Utilitarian style government with no more frustration, manipulation, deportation and retaliation. Rather a global purification without pollution causing contamination and intoxication. Just rehabilitation of the planet and civilizations. No more stupidity and greed, we the people must rise and change the documentation. Through smarter experimentation and concise argumentation don't get the wrong misinterpretation. We're going to overthrow the political leaders and dictators because it's time for an invasion. No more constant struggling and persuasion. Were just recreating a new industrialization like when Hitler's legacy fell because Russia used the proper stratification and didn't use evacuation. Lead Germany to believe they didn't have the proper papers of qualification.

They got too cocky and ended up making a miscalculation. Same goes for life, move forward or get put in the lazy categorization with the wrong affiliations, smoking the wrong medication. I got high off life by recreating, regenerating and making a difference in this place with a positive association. Not repeating that pointless weed inhaling. I don't feel bad for you and your dope fascination, grow up figure out your situation while me and my boys are laughing on vacation.

Printed in Canada

To foster caring and sharing within the community.

To reach the most vulnerable members of our society; guiding them towards happier, healthier, and more productive lives.

Our History

The Human League is a registered charitable organization (# 89307-2785-RR0001) in the City of Greater Sudbury.

The association was developed in October of 1996, by like-minded individuals who believed that all children should be given an equal opportunity to participate in and enjoy physical activity and healthy, nutritious meals.

you are crazy but that is because they gave up on their desires long ago. Prove to these people that anything is possible. I believe in you, just understand that mindset is everything. Once you understand this, you will harness the power to create your destiny. Do your research, develop a blue print that will enable you to build a self-sustaining platform in your life and start right in this moment! If something looks grueling, attack it as if you had no other choice with a smile on your face at all times. In doing this
I am certain you will be successful in anything you do."
– Connor LaRocque

Sponsored by the Human League Association

Phone: (705) 670-8633
Interested in donating call this number
Who We Are: The Human League is a not-for-profit organization based in the City of Greater Sudbury – home of the Breakfast Club for Kids, which provides local children with a nutritious breakfast every school day, and the P.L.A.Y. program; providing access to extra-curricular activities to children of low-income situations.

Our Mission

To promote the health, safety, and welfare of youth by removing social and economic barriers faced by children of lower-income families. To reach out to the most vulnerable members of our society, guiding them towards happier, healthier, and more productive live10s by subsidizing the costs associated with extra-curricular activities and developing programs and events designed to promote physical activity and healthy eating habits.

Our Objectives

To promote health, safety, and welfare among Canada's youth.
To teach parents and children the importance of goal setting, goal achievement, and motivation.

Inspiring Quotations

"Many people, especially ignorant people, want to punish you for speaking the truth, for being correct, for being you. Never apologize for being correct, or for being years ahead of your time. If you're right and you know it, speak your mind. Speak your mind. Even if you are a minority of one, the truth is still the truth."
– Mahatma Gandhi

"Measure yourself by your impact, not your income."
– Darren Hardy

"Don't be distracted by the criticism. Remember the only taste of success some people have is when they take a bite out of you."
– Zig Ziglar

"Walk away from the 97% crowd. Don't use their excuses, take charge of your own life. Life is a process of accumulation. We either accumulate the debt
or the value, the regret or the equity."
– Jim Rohn

"Somebody is in the hospital right now begging God for the opportunity you have right now, step into your moment."
– Tony Robbins

"I don't care who you are you have the power to change. The power to become the person you are dreaming of being. People are going to tell

Only we can help is what I'm trying to say, because
the good lord above would want it that way.

The power is now left with you the reader, what's your excuse?

What is life
By Monique LaRocque

It is the foundation of our existence, its forever changes always testing our resistance.

Who is to decide whether we eat to stay alive, or whether we starve, and fight to survive.

Who is to decide whether we have a roof above our heads, or a bed in the street, where most are found dead?

There is a sadness and pain that is lived every day, through the eyes of the children who constantly pray.

Pray for a life that is without struggle, for simple necessities for which we have no trouble.

Pray for a life that is without anger and hate, for the life they've been dealt; why is it their fate?

Pray for a life without hunger and sorrow, and hope there's a chance for a better tomorrow

Only we can help to a certain degree, to aid these people who have nothing to live comfortably.

Only we can help stop some of the crying, to ease some of the pain, and end some of the dying.